CATHOLIC
Etiquette

CATHOLIC
Etiquette

What You Need to Know about Catholic Rites and Wrongs

Kay Lynn Isca

Our Sunday Visitor Publishing Division
Our Sunday Visitor, Inc.
Huntington, Indiana 46750

Contents

To Joey, Jonathan, James, and Rachel.
And to my loving husband Joe, who introduced me to
Catholic culture.

Preface

riting this book has offered me an opportunity to find answers to many questions — both trivial and fundamental — that have gnawed at the edges of my conscience for years. Though I've been a "card-carrying" member of the Catholic Church for over ten years, and a student of Catholicism for fifteen years, I've still never quite felt comfortable with many of the rituals and traditions of Catholicism. I've always had the feeling that "real" Catholics could spot me as a newcomer, or outsider.

Perhaps some of this feeling stems from my personal experiences with insider and outsider status before joining the Catholic Church. Within my hometown, in Lutheran circles, I could have been considered an insider's insider. Raised in a small Midwestern city with a rich German Lutheran tradition, my roots in local Lutheranism reached back several generations on both sides. Nearly all of the many baptisms, weddings, and funerals I attended as a child and young person were for people raised in a similar tradition. My extended family was primarily Lutheran, most of my parents' friends and colleagues were Lutheran, and I spent twelve years attending Lutheran schools. By the time I reached adulthood, I thought I had a pretty good idea of what was expected at life's various milestones, at least within our local Lutheran milieu. Socially, if not intellectually, I felt at ease in Lutheran parameters.

My social confidence level dropped sharply, however, when I traveled to Japan and spent a year there as what the Japanese call a *gai-jin* (outside person). I blundered through many social occasions, wearing a bright yellow dress to a summer wedding, for example, when every other guest wore black. Trying to function in a foreign language and foreign environment, I made numerous daily mistakes in what I said and did. Much was forgiven, though, as I was immediately recognized as an outsider and therefore not expected to know all the customs and traditions familiar to those raised in that culture.

A more difficult and unexpected culture shock occurred when I left Japan and returned to my hometown to marry my Catholic fiancé. Expecting to be back in familiar territory, I found myself instead to be quickly immersed in an unfamiliar Roman Catholic culture. (The fact that my husband came from a different ethnic background in a large metropolitan area, and the fact that I flew in from Tokyo only a few weeks prior to the wedding, undoubtedly complicated things, also.) Although numerous guidebooks had been written and published to explain the nuances of Japanese etiquette to Westerners, I never found a guidebook to explain Catholic etiquette to Lutherans.

Thus, for the past fifteen years I've struggled to find the cues and understand the meanings and traditions of my adopted culture. Through my husband's work in the Catholic press, I've also found myself attending ceremonies and social functions with many members of the clergy and ecclesiastical hierarchy. Finally, after experiencing one too many frustrations, I asked my husband, "Why don't you publish a book on Catholic etiquette so somebody like me can figure out what to do?" He passed the suggestion along to his colleagues at Our Sunday Visitor. To my surprise, a few days later, the editor-in-chief called back and challenged me to write such a book myself.

So, through all my mistakes and confusion of the past fifteen years, I'm finally trying to figure out what contemporary Catholic etiquette really requires. Hopefully my journey will help others figure it out faster. I don't harbor any pretension of being a social arbiter. I have not served as Jacqueline Kennedy's social secretary (like Letitia Baldrige) nor do I come from a dynasty of etiquette mavens (like the Posts). Admittedly, I have never hosted (or even attended) an A-list party in Los Angeles, New York, Washington, or Tokyo. I am simply a curious observer who has tried to uncover answers to the daily complexities I have encountered, and am willing to share those discoveries with you.

Thank you to all who have helped guide me in this project, especially my family and friends. For several months, my family's patience has been taxed severely as I immersed myself in research and writing. My husband and four children have been eagerly anticipating the end of this book project, so I can begin to practice some household etiquette again, instead of merely writing about it. Thanks, too, to those who willingly shared their personal stories of etiquette problems and solutions with me, so that I could share them with you.

Readers who have comments, additions, questions, or corrections are invited to send them, c/o Our Sunday Visitor Publishing Division, 200 Noll Plaza, Huntington, Indiana, 46750.

Kay Lynn Isca
Fort Wayne, Indiana
September 30, 1996

Introduction

umerous friends and acquaintances, upon learning the title of this book, have looked at me with puzzlement and asked the same question: "Is there really a distinctly Catholic etiquette?" They find it hard to believe that there may be anything unique about etiquette practiced by or relating to Catholics, as opposed to those etiquette guidelines followed by considerate people of any faith.

This common reaction reflects both positively and negatively on the state of Catholicism — and the state of etiquette — in America today. On the positive side, it indicates that Catholics have permeated American society to an extent that we are no longer viewed as the separatist group we may have been considered a few generations ago. Today's American Catholics have been mainstreamed and accepted into all facets of contemporary American society, to an extent that we are now indistinguishable in most situations from our non-Catholic neighbors.

This honest response also reflects the more laid-back approach to etiquette common to the last few decades. Rather than memorizing a long list of "shoulds" and "should nots," many of us adopted a "let's all muddle through and just make the best of it" philosophy. We worked hard to promote a sense of inclusion, rather than exclusion, often preferring casual codes of dress and behavior to their more formal counterparts. If not carried to extremes, this relaxation of social rules has probably proved beneficial to most of us.

On the negative side, however, my friends' bewilderment reflects a limited awareness of some of the distinguishing characteristics of Catholicism — in doctrine, tradition, and devotional practices — and the protocol that stem from them. In an effort to avoid potential conflicts with our spouse, friends, or extended family members who may represent different faith traditions, we may all try sometimes to downplay Catholicism's religious and cultural distinctiveness. This one-size-fits-all style may work well in the business world, but it usually comes up short when applied to our religious or social lives.

When a significant event occurs — a birth, a death, a marriage, a family crisis, sometimes even a social invitation — radically different assumptions about "correct" protocol may suddenly surface. "What are we really expected to do in this situation?" we may find ourselves wondering, or at other times, "Why in the world would she do that now?" We may be startled to realize, too, that while a casual informality may work perfectly in some instances, on other occasions we need to be able to negotiate some of the traditional rituals and formalities after all. Perhaps, as we grow older, we may even gain a renewed appreciation for some of the protocol we disdained in our youth. The "oh, whatever" conduct codes of contemporary culture may suddenly appear woefully inadequate when we need to plan a funeral, for example.

Rather than exaggerate or downplay Catholicism's distinctiveness, we should simply recognize that an etiquette code specific to the Catholic subculture does exist, whether we follow it or not. Those of us who have ventured into the Catholic subculture as adults, either through marriage or other close personal contact with devout Catholics, will attest to an added etiquette layer within Catholicism that goes well beyond generalized guidelines. Some of the liturgical rituals and social duties associated with Catholic life may be comparable to those of other religious groups, but many are uniquely Catholic.

If we agree that a distinctly Catholic etiquette code exists, and that there may be a value in learning it, the next question might logically be, "How do I learn this code?" Unfortunately, that question is not so easily answered. In simpler times, a shared understanding of customs and decorum helped parishes and families reach a consensus regarding appropriate behavior for various situations. Then, these teachings were passed on from parent to child, from generation to generation, as occasions presented themselves.

Today, however, in our mobile and fluid society, families and parishes are more diversified, and relatives are often scattered around the country. Mingled communities, cultures, and faith traditions, as well as increasingly complex social issues, may frustrate our attempts to formulate or transmit any kind of succinct code.

In addition, the many social changes that have taken place both inside and outside of the Church in the past several decades have made it difficult to know just what current etiquette standards may be. The classic 1962 book *American Catholic Etiquette* by Kay Toy Fenner[1] seems amazingly rule-bound and quaint when read from today's perspective. Some of the attitudes and prohibitions expressed there may even astonish younger baby boomers and their offspring who've known only the post-Vatican II Church. Our elders, however, probably still remember many of these regulations, and may not always be certain about exactly which ones have been repealed and which remain in effect.

Secular etiquette books, too, from the same era, make most of us smile at their irrelevance for the majority of today's generation. When cleaning out a school library recently, I ran across some of these books from the early 1960's. The parents in the room at the time chuckled together as we flipped through a few pages, marveling at the amount of space devoted to the various do's and don'ts of glove wearing. The teenagers with us laughed uproariously.

Whatever our age, we all recognize that many of the etiquette rules our parents and grandparents lived by are no longer applicable to our lives. Yet, as we reach important milestones in our lives such as weddings, funerals, or baptisms, we may struggle with how to handle certain aspects of the occasion. Recurring issues, too, such as proper decorum at Mass, may leave us wondering what new guidelines (if any) have replaced the old. If we can no longer rely on family advice, then whom do we ask for guidance?

My hope is that this book will help fill that void. While I offer many suggestions and guidelines, you will undoubtedly find it less rigid and more option-oriented than comparable books of a generation ago. I've presented official Catholic teachings and policies wherever possible, but I've also tried to supplement those policies with personal life experiences.

In researching this book, I also uncovered some fascinating information about the history of some of the Church's sacraments and protocol. Learning the fuller meaning behind some of these ancient rituals has given me added appreciation for the liturgical life I share with Catholics around the world, and throughout history. By my sharing these discoveries with you, I hope you too may find a renewed appreciation for Catholicism's long and rich history.

Of course, not all aspects of Catholic protocol are universal. Regional, ethnic, and socioeconomic differences, as well as simple architectural differences, give us numerous local customs and etiquette variations from parish to parish. I've included some of these (though certainly not all), and have also tried to point out where such variations are most likely to occur. For the most part, though, I think you will find, as I did, that the commonalties between Catholic communities across the country are much stronger than their differences.

Whether you are a newcomer to Catholicism, a lifelong Catholic, or someone who is trying to relate more confidently with the Catholics close to you, I sincerely hope that you enjoy reading *Catholic Etiquette.* By taking the mystery out of some common Catholic practices, I hope to make it easier for anyone to participate more fully in the ceremonies which accompany Catholic life.

A Special Note to Readers Who Are Not Catholic

On behalf of Catholics everywhere, thank you for being interested enough in the topic of Catholic etiquette to pick up this book. My guess is that you have already had enough personal contact with Catholicism to recognize that there are definitely unique aspects of Catholic protocol not widely known to those raised outside the Catholic tradition. This book is one step toward bringing some of those hidden etiquette rules out into the open, hopefully making it easier for you to interact with those Catholics closest to you.

As former social barriers between Catholics and non-Catholics fall (one out of five Catholics in the United States is now married to a non-Catholic[2]), many of us have found ourselves floundering in "uncharted territory." While we appreciate opportunities to help our Catholic friends and relatives celebrate important times in their lives, we may easily feel intimidated as well. Unquestionably, many of the ancient ceremonies and rituals of the Catholic Church, and their related assumptions of appropriate decorum, can be daunting to the uninitiated. The explanations and behavioral guidelines offered here should help reduce the anxiety level for those of you who wish to attend a Mass, or participate in other Catholic ceremonies, but may have felt uncomfortable in the past.

While much of the discussion in this book is naturally geared toward practicing Catholics, I've tried to anticipate many of your concerns and address them also. The first two chapters particularly were written with you in mind. Throughout the book, each chapter gives hints for accommodating non-Catholic friends and family members in the celebrations, as well as tips for how best to include Catholic friends and family members in non-Catholic celebrations.

For those of you who would like additional information about Catholic teachings or sacraments, please check out the resources listed in the footnotes. While I realize that this book cannot solve all the etiquette dilemmas that inevitably arise as people of differing faith traditions live side by side, I pray that this book helps alleviate some of the more predictable misunderstandings.

Endnotes

1. Fenner, Kay Toy, *American Catholic Etiquette*. The Newman Press, Westminster, Mary.: 1962.
2. This statistic was provided by the Secretariat for Ecumenical and Inter-religious Affairs, and quoted in "Why Doesn't Daddy (or Mommy) Go to Church?" by Mary J. Bazzett, in the January/February, 1994, issue of *Catholic Parent* magazine.

Chapter One
Mass Fundamentals

For the devout Catholic, Mass attendance is a vital part of weekly, if not daily, life. It is the time when we gather together to come into God's presence, to be nourished in a special way by God and by one another. We listen to the words of Scripture, we pray together, and we share the ultimate soul food — the Body and Blood of Christ. Furthermore, we do all these things in a prescribed order, using many of the same words and rituals that have signified the Mass for nearly two thousand years.

Any discussion of Catholic etiquette, therefore, must begin with a discussion of the Mass — the cornerstone of Catholic ceremonial life. Baptisms, weddings, funerals, or any of the other special occasions we will examine in later chapters, can all be more easily understood if we first gain an understanding of standard Mass protocol.

Mass etiquette begins with a fundamental respect for the importance and sanctity of the Mass. An attitude of reverence should guide one's behavior at any religious service, but for

Catholics it is especially true. Why? A principal tenet of Catholicism, and one that distinguishes the Catholic Church from much of the Protestant world, is the belief in the Real Presence of Jesus in the Eucharist. For Catholics, the bread and wine do not symbolize or represent the spirit of Christ; they are changed into the Body and Blood of Christ during the Eucharistic prayer of the Mass.[1] From earliest childhood, Catholics are taught to show the utmost respect and reverence for this sacred and mysterious gift.

The simplification of the Mass rites that followed Vatican II stripped away some of the overt architectural and cultural references to the Real Presence. Any who worshiped in Catholic churches during the days of the Tridentine rite probably remember (maybe nostalgically) the awe created in part by the silence, the special language, and the decor. Today, though the atmosphere and rituals appear less formal (and less intimidating), a serious reverence for the divine presence in our midst remains a strong component of Catholic worship.

What does this mean for Catholics and our guests at Mass? At a minimum it asks us to ensure that our behavior (including our attire, our arrival, and our actions) will not detract in any way from the reverence accorded to the Mass. Worded more positively, it means that our choice of clothing and our complete comportment from arrival to departure should reflect an attitude of dignity and respect.

Let's look at how we demonstrate this basic attitude in a number of specific ways.

Attire

Choosing appropriate attire for Mass shows that we not only respect the importance of the Mass, but we respect our fellow worshipers as well, by avoiding any type of clothing that they may find distracting. While dress codes have been greatly relaxed in recent years, correct dress at Mass is still conservative and modest. Specific choices will vary, but, essentially, clothing appropriate to a typical business office would be similarly appropriate at Mass.

Mass attire also varies according to the occasion, the climate, the location of the parish, and the age of the majority of parishioners. Therefore, if you're going to be visiting an unfamiliar parish, don't hesitate to ask your host or hostess for advice about the local "dress code," or call the parish secretary and ask what people in that parish typically wear to Mass during that time of year. When in doubt, however, err on the side of "too dressy," rather than "too casual."

Adolescents and teens are usually given quite a bit of leeway in Mass attire, so Masses geared toward this age group invite fairly casual clothing. Most priests share the attitude that they are happy to see young people at Mass, and are only secondarily concerned about what they're wearing there. Young people should consider, though, the attitude they may convey with their clothing. Is Mass simply an afterthought, a brief "time-out" in an action-packed day, or is it a time specifically set aside for worship?

Some priests complain that many parishioners — adults as well as teens — now come to Mass dressed for what they plan to do after Mass (play golf, work in the yard, watch a ball game on T.V., etc.), rather than dressing with Mass as the primary focus. Consider making the extra effort to choose something to wear to Mass, then change clothes before going on to the next activity. You may find that it better reflects an attitude of respect for the importance and sanctity of the Mass.

A few specific items of clothing seem to be topics of such perennial concern that anyone writing about Mass etiquette is compelled to discuss them. Thus, while I hesitate to compile a list of do's and don'ts, I realize that some readers may want clarification on these issues, so I will give a few additional wardrobe guidelines.

Hats — Men never wear hats in Catholic churches, or in any Christian church for that matter. Women are no longer required to wear hats, but some older Catholic women who grew up in the days when head coverings were mandatory may feel more comfortable with a scarf over their heads. Though you will probably find yourself in the distinct minority by doing so (even on Easter), women may appropriately wear a hat inside a Catholic church at any time.

Ties — You may complain (or hear complaints from the men in your life) that a tie is uncomfortable and serves no useful function, but a tie does symbolize seriousness and respect in our society. In most parishes, therefore, a number of men wear suits and ties to Mass each week. An equal or greater number of Catholic men, however, opt for more informal Mass attire.

Shorts — Unless you're confident about the parish and its mores, wear slacks to Mass rather than shorts. Walking-length shorts can be appropriate for men or women at casual summertime Masses and in some resort areas, but are generally viewed as out of place at more traditional Masses.

Sandals — Women often wear bare legs and sandals at warm-weather Masses, but this practice may not be considered appropriate in all parishes. When in doubt, choose stockings. For men, bare legs and sandals are less common.

Jeans and sweats — In nearly every parish, you will find some people who routinely wear jeans to Mass. Although community standards vary, in most places this practice is tolerated but not encouraged. Some people make an effort to dress up their jeans by wearing a button-down shirt and perhaps a blazer with them. Others alternate between wearing sweatshirts and T-shirts with their jeans, switching from one to the other only when the season dictates. Wear them if you must, but realize that others may misconstrue your disdain for dressier clothing as disdain for the Mass. Sweatpants are only marginally acceptable, even at the most casual Masses.

Perfume and cologne — If a special scent is part of your trademark, please wear it subtly, or wait to apply it until after leaving Mass. Other Mass-goers may not appreciate having to inhale the various (per)fumes of those seated near them. Since my husband is allergic to several types of perfumes, I'm all too aware of how quickly a stranger's perfume or aftershave can trigger a debilitating allergic reaction.

Pagers and cellular phones — If at all possible, these modern communication gadgets should be left at home or turned off during Mass. A ringing phone or beeping pager detracts from the sanctity of the Mass, and can easily be distracting not only to the person carrying it, but to everyone else as well. Except for true emergencies, business calls should be able to wait at least until the conclusion of Mass.

Arrival and Entrance Protocol

Like our attire, our arrival time and our first gestures upon arrival should also reflect a reverent attitude toward the Mass. In most situations, arriving about ten to fifteen minutes early should be sufficient to allow parking and seating, and a brief silent prayer prior to the start of Mass. Some Catholics, however, prefer to arrive even earlier, to avoid feeling rushed, and to allow more time for silent meditation. Adjust your own arrival time according to your own preferences and the patterns of your parish.

On well-attended occasions, such as Christmas Eve, Easter, or First Communion, you may need to arrive at least thirty minutes before Mass is scheduled to begin in order to get a seat. Those who come later will likely have to stand throughout the Mass (or rely upon the charity of the earlier arrivals).

Unfortunately, in some parishes, parking lots remain empty until just five minutes before Mass, when hundreds of cars then pour in simultaneously. Fighting that kind of last-minute-rush traffic in the parking lot and at the door is obviously not the most reverent way to approach Mass. Allowing enough time to make a quiet and prayerful entrance demonstrates respect for the importance and sanctity of the Mass.

Upon entering a Catholic church, three gestures immediately distinguish Catholic worshipers from our non-Catholic counterparts: dipping our fingers into holy water, making the sign of the cross, and genuflecting. Non-Catholics entering a Catholic church need not attempt to imitate these gestures, but may instead just proceed quietly to a pew.

Each of these simple movements conveys a wealth of symbolism, but I suspect that this richness is probably unappreciated by the majority of Catholic participants. By learning more about the history and meaning behind these rituals, we can better understand their place and significance in the Catholic tradition. You may be surprised at how much your body language is saying.

Holy water — At the entrance to each Catholic church, we find some type of receptacle filled with blessed water. Traditionally, small bowl-like containers were placed or mounted near each church entrance. In newer churches, the baptismal font is often located near the entrance and doubles as the holy water font, also. As Catholics enter the church, we dip the tips of one or two fingers of our right hand into the water and bless ourselves.

In virtually every culture, water is associated with cleansing, often signifying spiritual as well as physical purification. In ancient times, Hindus, Egyptians, Babylonians, Greeks, Romans, and Hebrews all engaged in some form of ritual washings before entering their places of worship. As the early Christian church developed, Christian leaders, too, included a similar purification rite. In fact, as writer Tim Unsworth describes it, "Christians took water into their faith with such enthusiasm that Tertullian (A.D. 160-225) had to point out to them that one could pray *without* first washing one's hands."[2]

The earliest Christian churches included a porch or courtyard where people could wash before entering the main part of the church. Just as it had been used in preceding cultures, the ritual was a reminder to worshipers that they were entering a holy place. In today's society, modern plumbing has eliminated the actual need to wash in public, but the ritual drop of holy water still reminds us that we need to wash away secular things as we enter God's house.

Incidentally, although it is a common practice, we really should not bless ourselves on the way out of church. As author Kevin Orlin Johnson puts it, "You need to be cleaned on the way to the sacred mysteries, not on your way out to the sordid world."[3]

Over time, additional layers of meaning have also been incorporated into the holy water ritual. In contemporary Church teaching, touching the holy water is most often explained as signifying a renewal of our baptismal commitment. We dip our fingers into the water and touch them to our forehead, thereby repeating the gesture that first marked us as Christians. On varying levels of consciousness, the water reconnects us with this earlier spiritual gift.

The sign of the cross — Making the sign of the cross is a form of body language that instantly identifies someone as Catholic. In the entrance ritual, we use the one or two fingers just dampened with holy water to touch first our forehead, then the center of the chest, the left shoulder, and finally the right shoulder. This gesture is sometimes referred to as the large sign of the cross. At the same time we say silently, "In the name of the Father, and of the Son, and of the Holy Spirit. Amen."

In the Byzantine tradition, the sign of the cross is made either with two fingers (symbolizing the two natures of Christ — divine and human) or with three fingers (symbolizing the triune God.) A common Byzantine formula used while signing oneself is "Blessed is our God at all times, now and always and forever. Amen."[4] If you find yourself mouthing the more familiar formula too automatically, you may want to try substituting the Byzantine form occasionally.

What are we signifying by tracing the sign of the cross? Father Kenneth Ryan calls the sign "a visible profession of Christian faith in the Trinity and everything the cross of Christ means."[5] A Spanish bishop writing in the thirteenth century said the large sign of the cross represents the progress of Christ from the Father (head) to the Blessed Virgin (mid-body or womb) to heaven (right shoulder) by way of hell (left shoulder).[6] My guess is that few — very few — modern Catholics reflect on this progression as they make the sign of the cross. More prevalent is an understanding that it is a classic gesture of piety.

Genuflecting — Before entering the pews, Catholics traditionally pause and bend the right knee all the way to the floor, then rise up again. This act is called genuflection, from the Latin *genu flexo*, meaning "on bended knee." Some people include another large sign of the cross as part of the ritual. Like ceremonial washing, genuflection is an ancient mode of courtesy present in many pre-Christian cultures. The early Church embraced this gesture as an appropriate manifestation of respect for God.

As we genuflect, we point our bodies toward the tabernacle, a box-like container with doors, which houses the consecrated Hosts — the Body of Jesus. This special act of reverence is a sign of the Catholic belief in the Real Presence of Jesus. If no tabernacle is visible, then a genuflection in the direction of the main altar is appropriate. In Eastern churches, a deep bow is substituted for the genuflection, and you may see that occasionally in the United States, also.

Catholic liturgical law directs that a genuflection be made any time one passes before the Blessed Sacrament. Therefore, Catholics repeat this gesture as they leave at the end of Mass. What if we have to leave our seat during Mass, for example to take out a fussy baby, and return a few minutes later? Correctly, we should genuflect upon leaving and again upon returning, although that may be awkward under the circumstances. A brief bow toward the tabernacle should adequately satisfy etiquette guidelines in this situation, especially in today's more informal Mass atmosphere.

Seating — For the most part, you may sit wherever you like within the main seating area of the church. A few pews are sometimes reserved for the handicapped, for special guests, or for participants in a special ceremony, but these are usually clearly marked. If the church is especially crowded or if you are late in arriving, an usher can help you locate an open seat. With the exceptions of weddings, however, ushers do not formally escort people to their pews, but merely indicate where seating is available. Women typically precede their husbands or male guests into the pew, going in far enough to allow room for him, and for children or others who may be with them, to follow.

Early arrivals at a wedding or First Communion are entitled to keep the choice seats on the aisles so that they can see the proceedings better. (They earned this privilege by making the extra effort to beat the crowd.) At a regular Mass, though, those who are already in the pews should courteously move toward the center to make room for later arrivals, rather than force the newcomers to climb over them. Occasionally, there are valid reasons for wanting to keep your aisle seat — anticipation that you may need to leave early, for example. If that is the case, then step into the aisle momentarily to allow the new arrivals to enter the pew, then return to your seat.

Overcoats and accessories — Usually, you will have several choices about what to do with your wraps during Mass. Which one is most appropriate depends on your comfort, the weather, and the available seating.

Many modern churches offer a cloak room outside the main seating area where parishioners and guests may hang their wraps. If you choose to leave your overcoat(s) there, do so before entering the main part of the church. This would be an especially appropriate choice on rainy days (so you would not be bringing wet garments and umbrellas into the pews) and on days when the church is likely to be crowded (so you would avoid taking up potential seating space with your garments).

Some people prefer to keep their coats on during Mass. This is fine, especially if the indoor temperature is cool and you are more comfortable wearing your coat.

Perhaps the most common practice at many parishes is to remove a coat and place it beside us in the pew. If there is plenty of extra seating available, I don't see a problem with this practice, except perhaps that it conveys an attitude of rushing in and out of Mass as quickly as possible. If the church is particularly crowded, however, and certainly if you see any-one standing in the back, please take your coats into your lap or put them behind you to free up additional seating space. In crowded conditions, check to make sure that your hat, handbag, or diaper bag are not taking up potential seating space.

Let me share a personal incident that poignantly illustrates what I mean by observing seating etiquette at Mass. One Christmas Eve we were visiting my in-laws' parish in a rapidly grow-ing suburban area. The parish had already initiated building plans because they had outgrown their existing facility, so we were expecting the seating to be limited. We arrived early, but not early enough. All pews and even the overflow chairs were already filled when we arrived about thirty-five minutes be-fore the start of Mass.

Seven months pregnant at the time (and incidentally empa-thizing more and more with the Blessed Mother as the Christ-mas story was retold that year), I soon started to feel dizzy as well as uncomfortable while standing shoulder-to-shoulder with many others in a confined area. I kept anticipating that the priest or ushers would ask the congregation to try to make as much seating available as possible, by holding young chil-dren on laps, for example, and making sure that coats were not taking up seating space. I also expected the congregation to do these tasks without being asked, simply because they saw so many people standing.

Instead, the priest, ushers, and seated parishioners seemed

oblivious to the situation. In fairness, I did see one gentleman stand up and offer his seat to a frail-looking elderly woman near him. Otherwise, those seated seemed to feel pleased that they had seats (and their coats, babies, and diaper bags had seats, too) and unsympathetic to anyone who did not. "Is this a reflection of the spirit of Christmas?" I wondered with disappointment.

Finally, a sweet and empathetic young girl of about five or six years looked up and saw me standing near her. Without any prompting, she climbed up onto her startled mother's lap and offered me her seat. I gratefully sank into the chair and was immediately much more comfortable. In my view, her simple gesture is not only a classic definition of courtesy, it is a beautiful example of Christian charity as well.

General Decorum

As we've seen, Catholics express an attitude of respect for the sanctity of the Mass, and respect for the others around us at Mass, in various gestures. This respect is also manifested in our general comportment as we wait for Mass to begin, and throughout the service itself. Quietness, dignity, and attentiveness are key ingredients to appropriately reverent behavior.

This means that the main area of the church is not the place for socializing or chit-chat, even if the "action" has not yet started. Some Catholics hold a particularly high regard for the opportunity to pray in the presence of the Eucharist, and we should do nothing to interfere with their meditation.

It is certainly acceptable to nod or smile at acquaintances, or whisper a quiet "Hello" if a friend sits down next to us or in front of us. In the words of Emily Post, we should not, however, "carry on a prolonged conversation, giggle, gossip, or otherwise make ourself objectionable to others around (us)."[7] Introductions, too, should wait until after Mass has ended.

If we adopt an attitude of reverence and courtesy, it should be obvious that habits such as combing hair, applying lipstick, or other grooming necessities belong elsewhere. I laughed when I read the advice in the 1967 book *Christian Etiquette for Teenagers*[8] to "shun cleaning nails and giving manicures in church because this is a sign of disrespect." Can you believe, though, that just a few weeks later, as I was kneeling in prayer before the start of Mass, I heard the unmistakable sound of a nail clipper rhythmically doing its work in the pew behind me? Perhaps the obvious courtesies are not so obvious to everyone.

This brings up the question, "What do we do if someone seated near us is doing something inappropriate or distracting?" That is a difficult question and one I've struggled with myself. We will talk at length about young children at Mass in chapter three, so we can leave them out of the discussion here. (As a general rule, however, we should let the children's parents handle any discipline issues personally, even if we do not approve of their methods or limits.)

Another likely source of distraction is a group of teens or pre-teens sitting together without supervision. On occasion they may forget their manners and begin giggling or gossiping together. How do we handle the situation? The answer probably depends on how well we know the young people involved. If we know the kids and their families well, one discouraging word or gesture may solve the problem quickly.

More frequently, especially in larger parishes, the young people are likely to be strangers or mere acquaintances. In that case, I would advise forbearance (pray for it), or a move to a different seat if time and seating space permit. Later, we may wish to notify leadership personnel of the problem, either through a call to the church office, or a note to the pastor or youth minister. With teens, a word of advice from someone they know and respect is more likely to effect a change in behavior than a word by someone they do not know (especially if issued in front of their peers).

My own attitude is that I'm always grateful to see young people in church and that they should be encouraged rather than discouraged from attending. A harsh word to a sensitive teen could keep him or her away from the parish for months. As they gain maturity, these teens are likely to become more conscious of Mass etiquette and adjust their behavior accordingly.

Unfortunately, more and more frequently, the worst distracters at Mass are not children or teenagers, but adults. In this case, we can hold little hope that the offenders will simply "grow out of it." When adult Catholics show disrespect for the solemnity of the Mass, it is a more serious problem, and one without a simple solution. Several factors have contributed to this undeniable decline in proper reverence at Mass.

First of all, what we see at Mass is simply reflective of the general decline in courteous behavior in the broader society over the past several decades. When people do not practice common courtesy at home or at work, they are unlikely to be paragons of courtesy at church, either. If the "return to etiquette" movement of the last few years persists (and I certainly hope it will), then we should eventually see a corresponding improvement in manners at Mass, also.

Second, the changes in the Mass following Vatican II "muddied the waters" of etiquette expectations. Catholics soon learned that many familiar regulations and rituals had been repealed (mandatory head coverings for women and kneeling at an altar rail to receive Communion, for example), but were unsure what new procedures, if any, replaced them. It takes time for an etiquette code to adapt to new circumstances.

Third, Catholic elementary schools, while still vigorous in some places, are not the ubiquitous fixture in American Catholic culture that they were a generation or two ago. Graduates of the parochial school system, having spent years being drilled in the fine points of proper (and improper) Mass behavior, share a common understanding about expected decorum. It is a daunting challenge to CCD instructors to instill a comparable reverence for the Mass and its rituals in just a few hours per month.

So what can you do if you are bothered by distractive adult behavior at Mass? Primarily, you can set a good example yourself. When you model an attitude of reverence for the Mass and respect for your fellow parishioners, others may find they want to emulate you and/or have their children emulate you. If you have some specific concerns or suggestions, try writing a letter to your pastor about them. Perhaps a word from him in the bulletin or from the pulpit may raise people's awareness. Furthermore, if you feel strongly enough about wanting to improve manners at your parish, consider organizing some type of seminar, either through the CCD program or through a women's association, for example. Recruit an instructor, or if you're really ambitious, teach the class yourself.

Finally, if all else fails, please remember: While good manners are nice, they are not a prerequisite for being Catholic.

Endnotes

1. *Catechism of the Catholic Church*, English translation. Numerous publishers: 1994, no. 1413.
2. Unsworth, Tim, "Holy Waters Run Deep." *U.S. Catholic*, February, 1996, p. 50. Additionally, some of the other historical background on holy water is taken from this same article.
3. Johnson, Kevin Orlin, *Expressions of the Catholic Faith: A Guide to the Teachings and Practices of the Catholic Church*. Ballantine, New York: 1994, p. 200.
4. Cunningham, Lawrence S., "In the name of the Father. . ." *U.S. Catholic*. August, 1995, p. 50.
5. Ryan, Father Kenneth, *Catholic Questions, Catholic Answers*. Servant Publications, Ann Arbor, Mich.: 1990, p. 178.
6. Ibid., p. 177.
7. Post, Elizabeth L., *Emily Post's Etiquette*, 14th edition. Harper, New York: 1984, p. 193.
8. Carey, Floyd D., *Christian Etiquette for Teenagers*. Baker House: 1967.

Chapter Two
The Mass Liturgy

A prominent feature of the Catholic Mass, and one that distinguishes the Mass from many Protestant worship services, is how tightly most of the worship is scripted. With surprisingly little variation, on a given Sunday the same invocations, responses, sequence of readings, and prayers are recited in every Catholic church in the country. Furthermore, with little additional variation, these same words can be heard in Catholic churches throughout the world. Why is the Mass so consistent and predictable? The answer is found in the liturgy — the prescribed rites and ceremonies of public worship that are a fundamental part of Catholicism.

The most interesting definition of liturgy I've found is Father Thomas Richstatter's. He calls it "that ritual, repetitious, formal, symbolic, traditional, public, often incomprehensible 'stuff' that goes on in Catholic churches. . . ." Richstatter adds, though, that this "stuff" is an essential part of the Catholic heritage and moreover, a part of Catholicism that he particularly appreciates.[1]

Because Catholic worship is so liturgical, it can be especially confusing and intimidating to outsiders or newcomers. If everyone around us seems to be automatically doing, saying, and singing the same thing at the same time, but we don't "get it," it's easy to feel flustered and uncomfortable. We may even begin to think these specialized manners were deliberately designed to baffle and discourage the uninitiated!

In many Protestant churches, ushers distribute a worship bulletin each week to members and visitors as they enter the church. These bulletins usually list the order of service, and either quote the expected words of response or cite pages in a hymnal or other book where you can find the necessary information. Visitors from Protestant traditions may expect to find comparable written assistance when they arrive at a Catholic church, but this is not typical. Most parishes do have copies of *Today's Missal*,[2] a seasonal liturgy guide, available in the pews, but novices will need a helpful companion and/or considerable patience initially to learn how to follow it. Catholics who invite a non-Catholic guest to Mass, or spot someone looking lost in the pew next to them, need to be sensitive to this potential difficulty and offer quiet assistance when possible.

Catholics who've come to know the Mass liturgy well often find great comfort in its repetition. Once we understand the liturgy and our part in it, we can honestly feel at home in any Catholic church in the world. Wherever we travel, or wherever we may be transferred, we can be quite confident that there will be a Catholic parish nearby, celebrating the Mass each day in much the same way we're accustomed. This is indeed one of the marvelous treasures of Catholicism.

Understanding the liturgy involves more than just learning what to do so we won't feel foolish or out of place, however. Discovering, or rediscovering, the rich heritage and symbolism inherent in many of these words and gestures enables us to appreciate why these things are part of the liturgy. Take some time to focus on the liturgy more closely. You may find yourself feeling, as I have, more connected with Catholics throughout the world as you participate in these universal and time-honored rites.

Before we look at specific parts of the liturgy, two general characteristics of the Catholic liturgy deserve special mention. First of all, Catholic liturgy helps us worship God with our whole body, not just our head or voice. Physical movements — the standing up, sitting down, kneeling, making the sign of the cross, etc. — constitute much of what could be labeled "etiquette," or "protocol," for participating in a Catholic Mass. These are not just arbitrary rules, or postures of convenience, however. Each signifies an appropriate attitude that coincides with the action taking place. Putting ourselves into the prayerful postures of the liturgical tradition is an important non-verbal part of our dialogue with God.

The postures of the Mass are generally determined by national conferences of bishops, although individual bishops or pastors sometimes institute local variations. If we're visiting an unfamiliar parish, and everyone around us seems suddenly to be doing something we are unfamiliar with, then I suggest relying on St. Augustine's practical advice: When in Rome, do as the Romans do.[3]

Second, in Catholic liturgy, earthly elements — objects — are an integral part of the liturgy. In the words of writer Timothy McCarthy, "Just as the Word became flesh, so the word of God comes to us through bread, wine, words, oil, stone, and water. The word of God speaks to us through the interplay of these symbols. We, in turn, use the symbols to communicate with God."[4]

Those of us who come from a Protestant background, with a strong emphasis on the verbal and intellectual components of worship, may at first feel uneasy with some of these physical symbols that Catholics incorporate into the liturgy. Eventually, though, many come to appreciate these additional non-verbal means of expression, especially once their significance is understood. The style of Catholic worship asks us to use all of our senses — including taste, touch, and smell, as well as our sight and hearing — as we participate in the rites of the Mass.

Historical Background

As you might expect, the roots of the Catholic liturgy, including both the verbal and nonverbal aspects, are ancient. The structure of much of the liturgy originated in the Jewish prayer tradition, although the content naturally reflects the teachings of Jesus. The early Christians also modeled their buildings and many of their rituals on the Roman law court. As writer and researcher Kevin Orlin Johnson points out, "It isn't by coincidence that our rising up and our sitting down are so similar at Mass and at trials, or that you only find pews in churches and in courthouses."[5]

As early as the second century, the basic framework of the Mass and many of its essential elements were already well established in the Christian community. An account by St. Justin Martyr, written around the year A.D. 155, outlines what Christians of his time did when they gathered together "on the day we call the day of the sun."[6] Remarkably, over eighteen centuries later, the Catholic Mass today unfolds in just the same way.

If this format has been preserved intact since the earliest beginnings of the Christian church, why then do we talk about the dramatic changes in the Mass that took place recently following Vatican II? The answer to that question is too complex to be addressed in detail here, but essentially the liturgical reforms were part of a "back-to-basics" plan, a stripping away of extraneous details and decor.

Apparently, prior to the sixteenth century, there was considerable variety in the liturgical practices of the various dioceses and geographic regions of the Church. Then, in response to some of the criticisms and confusion immediately following the Protestant Reformation, the Church solidified the Mass liturgy into a format known as the Tridentine Rite, or the Roman Canon. For nearly four hundred years (from 1570 until 1969, when a new Mass order was published) the Tridentine Rite remained the official liturgy of the Roman Catholic Church. During the liturgical reforms of the Second Vatican Council, Church leaders were careful to maintain the historical continuity of the Mass, but also hoped to make the liturgy more "dynamic, simple, intelligible, and participatory."[7]

What changes actually occurred? The biggest liturgical change to come out of Vatican II was the switch to saying the Mass in the vernacular, the language of the people, rather than Latin. Another noticeable change moved both priest and altar to face the people, and removed the altar rails altogether. In addition, the Scriptures were returned to their original place of "paramount importance" within the Mass, and Church leaders began to request more liturgical involvement from lay people.[8]

Given this historical background, it is easy to see how Catholic Mass protocol remains steeped in tradition, but is also still developing in light of contemporary changes. With that in mind, let's look more closely at the basic rituals and practices we can expect to encounter at Mass. The Mass is composed of two basic parts: the Liturgy of the Word and the Liturgy of the Eucharist. These two main sections are preceded by brief introductory rites and followed by concluding rites. The rest of this chapter will follow this organizational outline.

Introductory Rites

As Catholics first enter the pew, after genuflecting in the aisle, we do not sit immediately. Instead, we kneel and pray silently. Kneeling is seen as a posture of both penance and adoration, and thus an appropriate posture as we enter God's presence. In most Catholic churches, a special wooden bench called a kneeler folds down from the back of each pew to make kneeling more comfortable, and to keep clothes clean.

The meditation and the introductory rites of the Mass serve

as a bridge from the everyday atmosphere to the sacred. As Archbishop Daniel Pilarczyk explains it, "We turn down the volume of our day-to-day stream of consciousness so that we can begin to hear the sounds of the sacred."[9] This is an important step in preparing for the Mass, and one that should not be overlooked or rushed. As we discussed in the previous chapter, we must also be careful not to intrude on other worshipers who are similarly trying to make this transition. After our own prayer is concluded, we sit.

Non-Catholics in attendance need not kneel, either now or at any point in the service. Simply remain seated, bow your head, and offer a silent prayer, if that is your custom. At any time during the Mass, if there is a part in which you do not wish to participate, simply sit quietly until that portion of the service is over. Unless you have health problems or some serious objection, however, it would be most appropriate if you stand when the rest of the congregation stands.

At the appointed time (and most Catholic Masses do start on time), the cantor, commentator, or another designated person will welcome everyone to Mass and announce the entrance hymn. At this point everyone stands (seen as a posture of respect and praise), and joins in singing. (Sometimes a prescribed short Bible verse, called an antiphon, is substituted for the opening hymn.)

During the hymn, the priest(s), altar servers, lectors, and other selected Mass participants process to the altar. The Lectionary (a beautifully bound book containing all the Scripture readings) is often held high during this procession and may be escorted by an acolyte (altar server) carrying a censer (dispensing incense), and/or two others bearing lighted candles. These are ancient ceremonial honors that used to be paid to Roman imperial dignitaries, or in their absence to the code of civil law that also embodied imperial authority.[10] Thus, these rituals honor the book, which symbolizes God's authority, not the priest, as visitors may mistakenly interpret. When they reach the area near the altar, these participants then place each item in its appropriate spot, and go and stand by their designated seats.

After the hymn, the priest opens the Mass with the words "In the name of the Father, and of the Son, and of the Holy Spirit." At this time, all present make the large sign of the cross (except non-Catholics) and respond, "Amen." According to liturgy expert James Schellman, the literal translation of the Hebrew word "Amen" is something like, "I will drive my tent peg into that," apparently a strongly affirmative phrase to desert nomads. Less literal translations are "So be it," or, "May it be so."[11] The priest and the congregation then exchange formal greetings.

The next step is the penitential rite. In this prayer, Catholics acknowledge our sinfulness and ask for intercession on our behalf. This is then followed logically by a plea for mercy, either sung or spoken. It is still common in some places to use the classic Greek words *"Kyrie eleison"* in place of the English "Lord have mercy."

During most of the liturgical year, the *Kyrie* is followed by the joyful *"Gloria,"* echoing the song of the angels on the first Christmas. The priest then reads the designated opening prayer, which gives the theme of that day's Mass.

Liturgy of the Word

Scripture readings — After the introductory rites, the congregation is seated for the Scripture readings. (After learning that for centuries the congregation remained standing for the entire Mass, I no longer take this opportunity to sit down for granted.) Usually lay lectors read the selected passages from the Old and New Testament, and a psalm is chanted or sung.

Since the Gospels (the New Testament books of Matthew, Mark, Luke, and John) present the words of Jesus, the Gospel lesson is given added respect. The congregation stands before the Gospel is read, and a priest or a deacon, rather than a lay lector, reads the portion of the Gospel assigned for the day. In addition, at the announcement of the Gospel reading, Catholics use their thumb to trace a small sign of the cross first on our forehead, then our mouth, and finally our chest. This is to indicate a desire that the Lord will be in our minds, on our lips, and in our hearts, as we hear the Gospel and then proclaim it by the lives we lead in the world.[12]

Homily — After the Gospel reading, the congregation once again is seated to listen to the pastor's homily. At this point our posture may convey more than we realize. As Lawrence Cunningham comments, "It always amuses me to watch people sit after reading the Gospel with an air of resignation. They seem to say to the priest shuffling his notes for the coming homily, 'Please try and keep my attention.' "[13] In light of this apt observation, perhaps an attentive posture during the homily could be added to our list of etiquette checkpoints. Catholic pastors usually expound on the Scripture lessons of the day and link them to our daily lives. Expect to learn something, and you may find your expectation fulfilled.

Creed — At the end of the homily, the congregation stands to profess our faith in the words of the Nicene Creed. This creed, first issued by the Council of Nicea in A.D. 325, summarizes the basic Catholic beliefs. At Masses for children, where few adults are present, the shorter and simpler Apostles' Creed is recited instead.

Intercessory prayers — The final rite of the Liturgy of the Word is the Prayer of the Faithful. At this time, specific and general prayer petitions are offered by a representative of the community, and the congregation responds to each with, "Lord, hear our prayer," or a similar response. The priest concludes the prayer and all of us again say together, "Amen."

Liturgy of the Eucharist

The Mass now moves toward its focal point — the celebration of the Eucharist. The Liturgy of the Eucharist has its roots in the Jewish family meal, but is modeled specifically after the Last Supper, where Jesus celebrated the Passover meal, then gave his disciples the instruction to "Do this in memory of me."

Gifts — We sit down for the first action in this half of the Mass, the presentation of the gifts. Selected members of the assembly — sometimes a family, sometimes the ushers — bring the bread and wine to the priest. At this time, also, ushers pass baskets or plates among the pews to collect the offering. Members of the parish have an obligation to contribute something, but the amount depends on personal circumstances of the parishioners and the needs of the parish. As the *Catechism* reminds us, "the faithful have the duty of providing for the material needs of the Church, each according to his abilities."[14]

Emily Post suggests an additional protocol: "Although there is no fixed rule about it, a husband generally puts the offering into the plate for both himself and his wife."[15] In my experience, this seems to be more of a personal and/or practical issue than an etiquette issue today. My husband often hands the envelope to one of the children to place in the basket, as a way of helping them see our offering as a family contribution, not just a spousal one. Choose whatever practice works best for you and your family.

Speaking generally about visiting Protestant or Catholic churches, Ms. Post also advises that, "When a man takes a woman friend to his church he may or may not contribute for both of them, but when a woman asks a man to go to a service with her they generally each make a contribution."[16] This would seem to be a reasonable and courteous practice to follow, although guests are not obligated to put anything in the offering basket at a Roman Catholic church.

When Catholics attend a parish other than our own, we should make a modest contribution when the offering basket or plate is passed, as a way of saying thank you to the church we are visiting. Also, while the larger part of our offering may go to that particular church, a percentage of it goes to the world-wide Church and helps in its support. When visiting a non-Catholic church, the same gesture would seem appropriate.[17]

Eucharistic Prayer — After the offering, the congregation stands as the priest begins the Preface of the Eucharistic Prayer. This is a short prayer of praise and thanksgiving, after which the congregation joins in reciting or singing the *Sanctus*, "Holy, Holy, Holy. . . ."

When the *Sanctus* ends, the congregation kneels, and the priest speaks the words of the Eucharistic Prayer. As part of the modern liturgical reforms, the priest now has a choice of several approved forms of the prayer. Each has a different tone and different antecedents, but all include the words spoken by Christ at the Last Supper.

It is during this Eucharistic Prayer that the high point of the whole Catholic liturgy takes place — the transubstantiation of the bread and wine into the Body and Blood of Christ. This is indeed the great mystery of our faith, as the prayer states. (Therefore, this is probably the least appropriate time during Mass to fumble in your purse for a tissue or take your preschooler to the potty. If at all possible, wait a few minutes until the Eucharistic Prayer has ended.) At the conclusion of the prayer, the congregation chants or says, "Amen." At this point we stand again, out of respect for the Monarch (Jesus) who has just come in.[18]

Lord's Prayer — We then begin the Communion Rite by praying or singing the Lord's Prayer together. Several prayer postures are commonly seen during this part of the liturgy. Our choice of which posture to adopt may be influenced by personal preference, and perhaps by the preference of those standing near us. Some families or couples join hands, and may reach out to join hands with those next to them, as well. Others extend their hands like the priest (a more charismatic posture). Many keep their hands folded in the traditional prayer gesture.

If you wish to join hands to emphasize familial unity, please do. Recognize, however, that some people near you may not feel comfortable with this posture. Look toward your neighbor and extend your hand, but do not urge anyone to grasp your hand if it seems clear from their body language that they prefer to remain "unattached." Likewise, if you dislike the ritual of joined hands during the Lord's Prayer, simply clasp your hands together and keep your eyes downcast. This should convey to your more gregarious neighbors that you do not care to join hands with them as you pray.

If you prefer to pray alone, but with extended hands, the situation is a bit more complicated because your seat partners could easily interpret your extended hands as an invitation to grasp theirs. If someone does misinterpret, or ignore, your signals, try not to let it bother you too much. Our focus should be on the prayer itself, rather than the posture.

By the way, the words which many generations of Protestants were taught to be the concluding words of the Lord's Prayer, "For thine is the kingdom and the power and the glory forever," were added to the Mass in 1963. They are not an integral part of the prayer, but a response by the people to the priest's prayer immediately following the Lord's Prayer.[19]

Sign of Peace — The next ritual is the Sign of Peace, when everyone in the congregation turns to the others nearby to exchange a handshake, or sometimes a kiss. (In most circles, the kiss is reserved for family members.) A common greeting is, "Peace be with you." During the Tridentine Rite, the sign of peace was limited to those around the altar, but Vatican II restored the earlier custom. Some older Catholics who spent many years attending pre-Vatican II Mass may still feel uncomfortable with this ritual. To some extent, each person can determine how much they wish to participate in this exchange (with immediate neighbors only or with those within a few steps reach, as well), but the preferences of your pewmates will affect you also. As with the joining of hands at the Lord's Prayer, it would be considered offensive to openly reject anyone's extended hand, but if you maintain a body language that says, "I prefer solitude right now," most people will respect your privacy.

Another reason older people may appear reluctant to participate in this ritual is due to certain health concerns. Several elderly women have complained to me about how painful a firm handshake can be against their arthritic fingers. Some strong and enthusiastic younger person who vigorously pumps neighboring arms during the exchange of peace may unwittingly inflict hours of pain on someone with serious arthritis. Therefore, be cautious about the amount of pressure you apply to your neighbor's hand, especially if he or she appears frail. Similarly, if you pick up signals that your neighbor does not wish to shake your hand, simply exchange a verbal greeting, and leave it at that. If you yourself have arthritis or a similar health problem, smile and exchange a greeting, but keep your hands at your sides to protect yourself. You are not obligated under these circumstances to shake anyone's hand or offer an explanation, either.

One final concern about this ritual I hesitate to mention, except that it seems so prevalent, especially during Midwestern winters. Have you ever sat behind someone who spent the entire Mass sneezing violently into his hands, only to have that person turn around at the Sign of the Peace and squeeze your hand and the hands of all your children, too? Frankly, I find this practice annoying and terribly inconsiderate. Unfortunately, I've never found a polite way to reject someone's extended hand, even if it's obviously coated with germs. If you have a bad cold, do everyone a favor by keeping your hands to yourself and offer a verbal Sign of Peace.

Distribution of Communion — After the exchange of peace, the priest prepares for the distribution and reception of Communion, with a mixture of both practical and symbolic gestures. While he is making these preparations, often with assistance from lay Eucharistic ministers, the assembly sings or chants the "Lamb of God." When the preparations are finished, the priest moves closer to the assembly, and he and his assistants begin to distribute the sacrament.

We kneel until it is our turn to come forward and receive the sacrament. Ushers often cue the assembly by moving from pew to pew to indicate when we should stand and step into line. As the people come forward, a hymn is often sung by the choir, and/or the congregation.

Kneeler etiquette — At this point, we should probably discuss some of the finer points of kneeler etiquette. (For those of us raised outside the Catholic tradition, this can be a puzzling piece of protocol.) After years of study and observation, I've reached several conclusions:

1) Whether we lower the kneelers when we first enter the church and leave them lowered throughout most of the Mass, or whether we lower them only as we need them seems to depend on our own preference — and the length of our legs.

2) When we get ready to go up to Communion, however, we need to return the kneelers to their raised position, as a courtesy to those who will be walking in that space. Only after everyone in our pew has returned to the row do we lower the kneelers and return to a kneeling position ourselves.

3) When sharing a kneeler with someone else, the basic protocol for who raises and lowers the kneeler roughly parallels current door-opening protocol. As with door-opening, the practice is not governed by simple rules, but requires some courteous intuition and common sense, too. In general terms, men often lower the kneeler for the women next to them, and younger adults often lower the kneeler for older adults. Children may courteously assume the responsibility of lowering the kneeler for their parents, as long as they can do so quietly.

4) Adults, too, need to exercise caution when lowering a kneeler. The sound of kneelers crashing against the floor (one author likened it to the guns of Navarone booming in the dis-

tance[20]) not only breaks the meditative silence, but focuses uncomfortable attention on the offender.

Receiving Communion — A more serious topic of etiquette, and one where the governing rules are necessarily much more strict, involves who may receive Communion at a Catholic Mass and who may not receive the sacrament. The National Conference of Catholic Bishops offers these stipulations for practicing Catholics: In order to be properly disposed to receive Communion, communicants should not be conscious of grave sin, have fasted for an hour, and seek to live in charity and love with their neighbors. Persons conscious of grave sin must first be reconciled with God and the Church through the Sacrament of Penance.[21]

Certainly one of the most difficult and painful problems for the Catholic Church today concerns Catholics who have divorced, then remarried outside of the Church. Church law bars these couples (living in what the Church terms invalid marriages) from receiving Communion. Before these Catholics can validly partake of the Eucharist, their marital situation must be resolved to the satisfaction of the Catholic Church. (Chapter seven discusses more fully the Church's teaching regarding divorce and remarriage.) The Catholic Church holds that this strict policy is the only way to maintain the sanctity of both the Eucharist and the Sacrament of Matrimony.

For all practical purposes, non-Catholics are also excluded from taking Communion at a Catholic church. (There is an exception listed in case of a "grave necessity," but it pertains only to extraordinary circumstances.[22]) Explaining their reasoning, the National Conference of Catholic Bishops says, "Reception of the Eucharist by Christians not fully united with us would imply a oneness which does not yet exist, and for which we must all pray."[23] Regardless of the practice of a particular Protestant church, Catholics are similarly prohibited from taking Communion when visiting a non-Catholic church. Catholics who invite non-Catholics to Mass have an obligation to clarify this policy with their guests prior to Communion, so that no uncomfortable situations arise suddenly during the reception time.

For those who cannot (or for some reason do not care to) receive Communion, simply remain seated in the pew while others go forward. If you are sitting in the middle of a pew, try to position your legs so that your pewmates may walk past without too much difficulty. If you are sitting on the aisle, it may be easier to step into the aisle to let your neighbors pass, then return to your seat. At any given Mass there are usually a number of people who do not go forward to Communion, so you need not feel uncomfortable.

Those who are receiving the sacrament usually will be permitted to choose reception in the hand or directly on the tongue. If Communion is to be received in the hand, one hand should be placed on top of the other in the form of a cross. After the minister places the Eucharist in the hand, the communicant then places the Host in his or her mouth. Those who wish to receive on the tongue, should tilt their heads back slightly and put out their tongue. (Or as Father John Kenny explains, "You offer your tongue not quite as dramatically as you do when having your throat examined."[24]) The minister will then place the Host on our tongue. The communicant then makes a large sign of the cross while facing the altar. A third manner, used in the Eastern Churches (both Catholic and Orthodox), is called intinction. In this method, the priest dips the Host into the chalice, then places it directly on the tongue of the communicant.

Prior to Vatican II, Communion in the Roman Rite was always received on the tongue, and some Catholics strongly disapprove of reception in the hand. The primary concern is that the Host may not be consumed immediately, thereby desecrating the Body of Christ. Given the Catholic belief in the Real Presence of Christ in the bread and wine, it would be seriously offensive to do anything other than put the Host into your mouth the moment you receive it.

Since Vatican II, a minister usually also offers the Blood of Christ to communicants from a common chalice. (In the Tridentine ritual, the priest alone drank from the chalice and only the Hosts were offered to the congregation.) Church leaders have made the use of the cup optional, however, because many persons are passively against the use of the cup for hygienic reasons.[25] Unlike some Protestant groups, the Catholic Church teaches that the whole Christ is present under either form, making it unnecessary to receive the Eucharist under both species.

After receiving the Holy Eucharist, the communicants return to their pews and kneel, spending a few moments in personal prayer. Remember to maintain a reverent posture and solemn silence here, even though it is almost time to go home. One author commented that some people "have a quick chat with God, and immediately sit back in their pew and look around as if it were intermission at the theater."[26] Others seem to think this time is for zipping coats and getting out the car keys, in anticipation of a quick getaway. Although parish customs vary somewhat, it is most appropriate to remain kneeling until the priest returns to his seat. At that time, we sit back and raise the kneelers a final time.

Concluding Rites

The concluding rites of the liturgy are brief. The assembly stands while the priest offers a short prayer and a blessing, then tells us, "The Mass is ended." Although at this point my young nephew has been known to shout "Yes!", the correct response from the congregation is, "Thanks be to God." Most times a final hymn is sung, while the priest and participants leave the altar. When the hymn is over, we leave quietly, genuflecting again as we leave the pew. As mentioned earlier, it is not necessary to repeat the holy water gesture on your way out, although many Catholics do so.

Having been spiritually renewed and nourished, we are ready to go out into the world again. As Archbishop Daniel Pilarczyk writes, "The remembering, the offering, and the sharing are all directed toward transforming the life we take up again outside church. . . . The Mass is the center of our lives, not because it takes us away from our worldly involvements, but because it empowers us to deal with those involvements in the name and with the energy of Christ himself." [27]

Endnotes

1. Richstatter, Thomas, O.F.M., *Liturgy! Why I Go to Church.* Abbey Press FaithNotes, St. Meinrad, Ind.: 1991.
2. *Today's Missal: Masses for Sundays and Holy Days with Daily Mass Propers for the Liturgical Season.* . . . Oregon Catholic Press, Portland, Ore.
3. Johnson, Kevin Orlin, *Expressions of the Catholic Faith: A Guide to the Teachings and Practices of the Catholic Church.* Ballantine, New York: 1994, p. 66.
4. McCarthy, Timothy G., *The Catholic Tradition Before and After Vatican II, 1878-1993.* Loyola University Press, Chicago: 1994, p. 208.
5. Johnson, pp. 170-71.
6. *Catechism of the Catholic Church*, English translation. Numerous publishers: 1994, no. 1345.
7. McCarthy, p. 215.
8. Ibid., p. 217.
9. Pilarczyk, Archbishop Daniel E., *Understanding the Mass.* Our Sunday Visitor Publishing Division, Huntington, Ind.: 1987, p. 10-11.
10. Johnson, p. 62.
11. Schellman, James, "Let the Church Say Amen." *U.S. Catholic*, April, 1996, p. 62.
12. Stravinskas, Rev. Peter M.J., *The Catholic Answer Book 2.* Our Sunday Visitor Publishing Division, Huntington, Ind.: 1994, p. 170.
13. Cunningham, Lawrence S., *Catholic Prayer.* Crossroad Publishing, New York: 1989, p. 60.

14. *Catechism,* no. 2043.
15. Post, Elizabeth L., *Emily Post's Etiquette,* 14th edition. Harper, New York: 1984, p. 193.
16. Ibid.
17. A new book, *How to Be a Perfect Stranger: A Guide to Etiquette in Other People's Religious Ceremonies,* may help you feel more comfortable. (Edited by Arthur Magida, Jewish Lights Publishing, Woodstock, Vt.: 1996.) The treatment is somewhat uneven, with some denominations presented more clearly than others, but it is a useful compendium.
18. Johnson, p. 66.
19. Ryan, Father Kenneth, *Catholic Questions, Catholic Answers.* Servant Publications, Ann Arbor, Mich.: 1990, p. 85.
20. Meara, Mary Jane Frances Cavolina, et al., *More Growing Up Catholic.* Doubleday, New York: 1986, p. 60.
21. *Today's Missal,* inside cover.
22. *Catechism,* no. 1041.
23. *Today's Missal,* inside cover.
24. Kenny, Father John J., *Now That You Are Catholic: an Informal Guide to Catholic Customs, Traditions, and Practices.* Paulist Press, New York: 1973, p. 16.
25. Ryan, p. 52.
26. Meara, Mary Jane Frances Cavolina, et al., *Still Catholic After All These Years.* Doubleday, New York: 1993, p. 5.
27. Pilarczyk, p. 30.

Chapter Three

Children at Mass

hildren and church are not always a match made in heaven. The solemn silence and reverent decorum inherent in the Mass and its liturgy can easily be shattered when a few dozen vocal and rambunctious children of varying ages are included in the congregation. While we kneel in prayer, a baby may wail inconsolably. Perhaps we sit attentively to listen to the Scripture or homily, only to hear instead a tantrum, bickering siblings, or parental discipline taking place in the pew in front of us. As we leave our seat to go up and partake of the Holy Eucharist, we may feel the irritating crunch of Cheerios beneath our feet or witness an unsupervised preschooler doodling in the hymnal. Needless to say, it is difficult to remain focused on the sacred during these circumstances. Moreover, if we are the ones directly responsible for keeping these children from being disruptive forces during Mass, while simultaneously trying to meditate ourselves, we may find Mass time characterized more by tension than by prayer.

Do children belong at Mass? Church law states explicitly that once children have made their First Communion, they too, have an obligation to fulfill the precept of Mass attendance on Sundays and Holy Days.[1] In the modern Catholic Church, First Communion is celebrated in the second grade, or at about seven years of age. By this age children are expected to understand enough about moral responsibility (and good behavior) to participate in the Mass on a regular basis.

Church law speaks less directly about children's place at Mass for the years preceding a child's First Communion. The *Catechism* cites "the care of infants" as one of the few legitimate excuses for missing Sunday Mass,[2] but I do not think we should interpret this to mean that infants are therefore unwelcome at Mass. Many Catholic parents find they need and appreciate the Mass in a special way during the challenging months immediately following the birth of a child. Rather than banish these families from the Mass, the parish should support and encourage their efforts to attend and participate.

A relevant Catechism reference tells us parents have an obligation to "initiate their children at an early age into the mysteries of the faith . . . and associate them from their tenderest years with the life of the Church."[3] When combined with Jesus' familiar admonition, "Let the children come unto me,"[4] Catholics seem to have a clear mandate to bring children to church long before they are ready to make their First Communion.

How can we include youngsters at Mass while still respecting Mass etiquette? This is the key question that this chapter will address, and a question I have been struggling with personally for nearly eleven years. Unfortunately, I cannot offer any guaranteed solutions, but only suggestions and considerations. Each child is a unique gift from God, with his or her own temperament, inclinations, and needs. What works perfectly for one family, or even for one child within that family, may not work at all for a different child. Even more bewildering is when some technique works perfectly one week, only to fail completely the next.

Typical problems change as the child matures, so sugges-

tions and concerns are grouped into several age categories —
newborns, older infants, toddlers, preschoolers, and pre-First
Communicants. Before we look at etiquette expectations for
parents of these children, though, I would like to mention some
special etiquette considerations for those adults who have no
young children at home.

Adults with No Young Children

It may be tempting to think, "My child certainly *never* acted
that way in church," or even more tempting to project, "I *would*
never let my child do that." Maybe an exasperated "Can't they
control that child?" has entered your mind more than once
during Mass. Instead of being quick to judge or criticize, however, try to offer families with young children your moral support. Pray for the youngest members of our parish and for their
harried parents as well. This may well be one of the most difficult yet important times in their lives, and one where spiritual
support may be crucial. Yes, it can be hard to feel spiritually
nourished after attending Mass surrounded by young children.
Just remember, it is probably even more difficult for the parents themselves to receive such spiritual nourishment.

If you find yourself particularly distracted by children at
Mass, experiment with attending Mass at different times. Some
Masses are much more popular with parents of young children
than others, so you may be able to minimize your interaction
with them by attending an alternative Mass. You may find, too,
that sitting in a particular part of the church may be more con-
ducive to contemplative prayer. For example, the front row
center is a spot most parents with troublesome children avoid.
You can see only the priest and altar in front of you and may
gain some distance from the youngsters.

Although you may appreciate those moments when you can
pray in the Real Presence, Mass is not really about private
meditation. The Mass is primarily communal worship and participation in the Eucharist. If you want to meditate, try adding

another meditation time to your week. Most Catholic churches have chapels or other meditation areas, often open twenty-four hours, where you should be able to avoid distractions and interruptions. Parishes also regularly offer weekday Masses, which attract much smaller crowds and few children.

Most of the complaints voiced about the misbehavior of children at Mass are directed toward the parents of those children. Parents may be viewed as lax in discipline or inconsistent in their expectations, and to some extent these characterizations may be true. What you may be forgetting, though, is that these same parents have already shown a considerable amount of self-discipline just in getting to Mass. Please show some empathy and respect for the adults who go to the trouble of getting all the family members washed, dressed, and delivered to Mass on time, sometimes with no help from a spouse. It is certainly much easier to stay home and skip Mass altogether. Your attitude and demeanor toward that family, whether you realize it or not, may mean the difference between whether they come back again next week or not.

I remember one Sunday morning when my husband was out of town and my three boys were very young. We had moved to the area only a few months before and were new to the parish. The parish was new also, meeting in a temporary location in an elementary school auditorium, and no cry room or nursery was available. My oldest son was two years old and my twin boys were about six months old.

I toyed with the idea of skipping Mass that weekend, but finally decided to take my children and try a solo outing. Just getting the kids out of the car and into the school was a challenge. A diaper bag slung over one shoulder, I carried a baby in an infant seat under my arm with the other baby strapped into a Snuggli carrier I wore on my chest. My toddler held onto my pocket as we waddled into the school.

Eventually, I settled into a folding chair, with my toddler next to me and the infant seat on the floor between my feet.

Almost immediately, the boys started fussing. I tried to soothe the babies by jostling the infant on my chest with one arm while rocking the infant seat with my foot. With my one free arm, I struggled to restrain my toddler. Inevitably, my efforts at quieting the three boys were sometimes successful, sometimes not. By the end of Mass, tears of frustration and embarrassment were threatening to spill down my face. Mentally chiding myself for even attempting to go to Mass on my own, I tried to make as inconspicuous an exit as is at all possible with three babies. Before I could sneak out the door, however, an older woman touched my arm. I began mumbling an apology, but she stopped my words. "*Never* apologize for bringing children to church," she stated emphatically. "My own daughter rarely attends Mass any more because she says it's too much hassle with the children. This pains me. I was not sitting near enough to you to be able to offer you a hand with the babies during Mass, but I wanted to come over and say, may God bless you and your family. God bless you for making the effort."

I doubt if she was expressing a unanimous opinion of the people seated in Mass with us that morning, but she strongly influenced my mood not only on that day, but many times during difficult Sundays that followed. Though I never saw that woman again, she left me feeling much less defeated and more confident that taking my children to church with me was God-pleasing, if not always pleasing to everyone else in the congregation. Many times since, when I find myself getting irritated with my own children or somebody else's children, her words come back to me: "God bless you and your family. . . . Never apologize for bringing children to church."

Infants

If parents and the parish make some allowances for babies, newborns should not pose a major problem in church. Young infants typically sleep through much of the Mass, are not mobile yet, and are often content to gaze around at the new faces and lights. If newborns do start to fuss, they can often be soothed by shifting positions, or by offering them a pacifier or bottle of water or milk. A crying baby, however, is undeniably a distraction to everyone present. If you cannot quiet the baby within a minute or two, please exit with the baby as a courtesy to the others at Mass.

For breast-fed babies who are hungry, I suggest mothers retreat to a quiet corner outside the main seating area of the church. (Feel free to ask an usher to provide a chair for you if one is not readily available.) No matter how comfortable you feel about nursing, and how completely natural an action it is, there are those who may be distracted or offended by this activity during Mass. In some ethnic parishes, nursing in the pew may be considered perfectly acceptable, but in mainstream American parishes more discretion is advised. Those mothers who are particularly skillful at concealing the process can probably be granted some additional leeway, as long as they remain aware of those around them and sensitive to potential reactions.

If you do notice someone discreetly nursing an infant in the pew, however, try not to take offense. Privacy standards regarding nursing in public vary considerably, depending upon our ethnic, social, and family backgrounds. The nursing mother may have no awareness that her actions could possibly be considered offensive.

If your baby is simply fussy, sometimes you need only carry him or her as far as the back of the main seating area. I spent many minutes standing and swaying behind the last pew with my infant daughter in my arms. She was quiet and I felt more a part of the Mass than when I retreated further. (On a practical note, wear comfortable shoes if you can expect to stand holding a child for most of the service.)

If the baby is still noisy in the back of the church, your next option will be somewhat determined by your local parish and its architecture. Many modern parishes have glass-enclosed "cry rooms" or a large gathering area separated by glass partitions from the main seating area. Usually speakers transmit the sounds from the priest's microphone into the room, although the din sometimes makes it difficult to hear. (Humorist Kevin Cowherd claims the noise level in the cry room at his parish rivals that of the Concorde at take-off.[5]) If the parents encourage some discipline in the cry room or gathering area, rather than tolerating complete pandemonium, this option does offer an opportunity for limited participation in the Mass, without disrupting others.

If no cry room or partitioned area is available, then your options are more limited. When our oldest son was an infant, we attended a parish whose building was one hundred fifty years old. It was a magnificent structure, but one obviously not designed to accommodate screaming children. There was only a small vestibule area, with the oak doors to the main seating area always kept open. I often took my fussy baby out there, but would soon be outside or out in the car, because his cries reverberated off the massive walls and echoed through the whole church. (It was not until about a year later that we novice parents realized we had unwittingly taught our clever young son a pattern: act loud and cranky during Mass and you can go crawl in the grass or read stories in the car; act quiet and you will be forced to sit still and be bored.)

Sometimes parish options are available, but not obvious. An usher at a small but friendly parish I once visited suggested I sit with my baby in the pastor's office, which had speakers through which I could listen to the Mass. Though I felt I was intruding on the pastor's private space, it did solve the problem that day for me and the rest of the congregation. If you are new to a parish, or new to parenting, feel free to ask another parent or call the church office and ask the receptionist what facilities may be available for you and your baby. If you think your parish could do more to provide a designated area for parents and babies, talk to your pastor. Perhaps you could creatively convert some small space for that purpose.

In addition to crying, infants have a couple of messy habits I hesitate to mention, except that they can pose etiquette concerns at Mass, also. As any veteran parent knows, young babies frequently spit up, some babies more often than others. Most often the liquid lands on Mom's lap or Dad's shoulder, but unfortunately it can land elsewhere, also. If your baby is a frequent spitter, try to protect the pew by keeping a blanket or burp cloth under your baby. I've watched babies spit up on an upholstered pew during Mass, and have been disheartened to see a nonchalant parent ignore the mess or simply dab at the spot superficially. Mass etiquette probably does not demand that we carry and use a spray disinfectant, but a damp washcloth in a zip-lock bag might be a good idea for such situations. If your baby spits up on the seating and you cannot clean it effectively yourself, mention it to one of the ushers as you leave, so that it can be cleaned up before the next Mass.

Another topic which may seem too obvious to mention is diapers. If you must change your baby's diaper, please do it in the restroom. You may view this procedure as a simple and natural function, but the process is distracting and potentially messy. Better to excuse yourself for a few minutes and take care of the diaper in an appropriate place than to have some kindergartners being "grossed out."

Since we've established that there are definitely times when it is most appropriate for us to take our infants out of Mass, we may also wonder if there is any special protocol for leaving and returning to our seat again. While no formal protocol exists, a few considerations should be kept in mind in order to minimize any further disruption of the Mass.

First, please try to limit the number of times you leave and return. After a couple of back-and-forth trips (the baby is calm in the back of the church, but begins to fuss again a few minutes after returning to the pew. . .) it's best to stay out until

Mass is ended. Repeated coming and going, especially if practiced by several families simultaneously, can be quite distracting. One December Sunday, as I was standing in the back with my baby, the traffic passing through the doors during Mass reminded me of the parade of holiday shoppers hurriedly going in and out of a department store.

Second, reenter sensitively. In the Lutheran tradition in which I was raised, we were taught to enter only during the singing parts of the service, never the spoken. Catholicism does not seem to have a similar prohibition, but we can still be sensitive to the timing of our reentry. Be careful not to disrupt prayer or the Consecration or the reading of the Gospel, for example.

Older Infants

As infants gradually become more mobile, vocal, and active, the difficulty in confining them at Mass increases, too. This is also when differences in temperament begin to become more visible. Some infants at this stage are content to sit on a parent's lap or rest quietly in an infant seat of some type, and observe the action around them. Others are naturally more active and therefore more of a challenge at Mass.

One of our children was an eager explorer who wanted to investigate everything around him — screws, bolts, neighboring handbags, aisles, etc. My husband and I used our own bodies as physical barriers to restrict his movements as much as possible, but we really never did find a way to confine him effectively during this phase. Our daughter was very sociable, and an equally challenging older infant at Mass. She wanted to make friends, share toys, chat, and crawl into the laps of strangers. The only way we found to keep her at this age from interacting with everyone around her was to remove her to a remote corner.

Experiment with bringing some soft toys or cloth books to Mass, but be leery of anything with rattles or bells or squeaks. Some children will be absorbed by such diversions; others (like mine) will prefer to investigate the people and things that weren't brought from home. Teething rings were one item I usually tried to bring along — until one of my boys decided to fling his across the aisle and beaned a nearby parishioner. After that, we rarely brought any toys to Mass.

Be conscious, too, of how you or especially how older siblings try to entertain baby. Sometimes in the interest of keeping an infant absorbed, a sideshow act of funny faces and mimed games takes place. My five- and seven-year-olds tended to forget their Mass manners completely when faced with the task of keeping their baby sister amused. We finally had to enforce a "parents only" rule about caretaking during Mass.

As you may have already discovered, this stage of child development can test parents' patience and creativity during Mass. Unless your parish has special staffing and infant-care arrangements, these children are probably still too young to be left in the nursery. Look around to see how other parents are handling children of about the same age and you may pick up some ideas. Recognize, though, that your child's personality may demand different solutions. Realize, too, that your child is quickly moving toward the toddler phase, when a different set of parenting strategies is likely to be needed.

Toddlers

The toddler stage is unquestionably the most difficult Mass phase for parents to negotiate. Toddlers by nature do not like any kind of restraint. They want to run, jump, eat, yell, explore, ask questions, and announce their bathroom needs whenever and wherever they wish. Not many toddlers I've ever met are content to sit quietly for an hour without complaint. So what are your options? There are several, each with its own advantages and disadvantages.

In the pew — Some parents prefer to keep their children with them at Mass, from babyhood throughout their childhood. Betty Galvano, a mother of six, writes, "Having my family together in church as much as possible, although it was a nuisance, has made us much closer."[6] This strategy also eliminates the problem of weaning a child away from the play room at a later stage. If the child has been brought into the pew from his or her earliest days, the thinking goes, the child will not resist as he or she matures.

This choice obviously works well for some families, but I cannot recommend it to every family. Not every parent has the patience and tolerance level to cope with a toddler at Mass on a weekly basis. Not every child will fall readily into a disciplined church routine, either. If you find that you and your child both dread going to Mass, or that you and your spouse frequently spend the time after Mass arguing about the children's behavior, then it's time to switch strategies.

Whether you choose to bring a toddler into the pew with you each week or just on occasion, some pre-planning will help minimize (but probably not eliminate) problems. Always bring along a bag that includes dry diapers or underpants and a change of clothes, just in case. As you choose a seat at Mass, plot your escape route, again just in case you need it. Though at least one expert advises parents of toddlers to pick a seat near the front so the children can see better,[7] this is a gutsy move, and frankly not one that worked well for us. When my children were toddler age, I felt much more comfortable sitting where we were less on display and where I could make a less noticeable exit if necessary.

What else should parents bring? First, let me address what *not* to bring — food. One of my pet peeves is parents who feed their kids breakfast and/or snacks during Mass. Infants who must eat every few hours are one thing; toddlers swinging bottles or sippy cups and dripping sticky liquid all over the floors, seats, and adjacent coats, purses, etc. are a different story. Parishioners who attend a later Mass should not have to feel like moviegoers who follow a kiddie matinee at the local theater. It upsets me, too, when I have to take my kids out of

Mass only because they are whining about wanting someone else's snacks.

Allowing our toddlers to nosh their way through long car rides or soccer matches of older siblings is something we've all tried. Church is a separate place, though, with different rules and a different attitude. Feeding snacks to a toddler may be an easy way to keep him/her seated and occupied at Mass, but it should not be considered appropriate. I would encourage pastors to inform their parishioners (with a posted sign if necessary) that food and drink are no longer allowed in the main seating area.

What about bringing toys and books to Mass? This depends upon your child and how he or she typically plays. Again, be aware not only of your own child, but also how your choices may affect another child who is not allowed to bring toys to Mass, or who may want to join in playing against the wishes of the parents. If a toy must be brought, a Magna-Doodle or Etch-a-Sketch type toy is the best I've seen for being quiet, unobtrusive, and clean. Any robots, dinosaurs, trucks, or fire engines almost always seem to bring out the required sound effects, and end up being a problem to you or to those around you. The ubiquitous Barbie dolls are not usually too disruptive — until everyone in the family starts the inevitable search for the minuscule lost accessories.

Books (preferably religious ones) can be a good choice if your child will sit quietly and look at the pictures. If your child expects you to read the book, however, leave it at home. I've been seated near enough adults reading Doctor Seuss or Clifford books "*sotto voce*" in Mass to say first-hand that it can be irritating to those around you.

Crayons may work for some toddlers, but not many. It's too easy to add crayon markings to pews and/or hymnals along with their coloring book. By the time children can be trusted with crayons, they are too old to be bringing them to church.

Writer Ann Ball remembers fondly how her grandmother

used to wordlessly fold her handkerchief into a Baby Jesus in swaddling clothes, and hand it to the young Ann. Maybe it's an old-fashioned idea, but that's the kind of "toy" I prefer to see in Mass.[8]

In summary, if you wish to keep your toddlers with you at Mass, more power to you. If you make this choice, however, recognize that you have a responsibility to your children and to the others around you to instill in your children the idea that Mass is different and that we behave differently there than we do in secular situations. This means food, drink, and distractive playthings are left at home, and quiet and reverent behavior is encouraged at all times.

Nursery — For some people, a room or space dedicated to keeping toddlers content while their parents attend Mass is a godsend. Many modern parishes have a safe play area set aside for toddlers and preschoolers, equipped with a variety of toys, and staffed by a paid employee or volunteers. The parents can drop the children at the nursery, then worship together without the pressures of disciplining their children, or the discomfort of feeling that their children are disrupting the Mass. Other parishioners are spared the occasional tantrums and tears, as well.

For all four of our children, we relied quite heavily on the church nursery from the time they were about eighteen months of age (or when we discovered the nursery at our new parish) until they reached about three years of age. (From ages three to four, we made use of the nursery occasionally, then eliminated it as an option after the children turned four.) My husband and I looked forward to the hour respite from intensive child care and really appreciated the opportunity to focus on the spiritual dimension of the Mass.

Some children and families adjust to the separation idea more easily than others, of course. We introduced the idea to our children as we paced the hallways with them as infants. They saw children playing, and we presented the room as a "big-kid thing." At about one-and-one-half years, or when we thought they were old enough, we attempted to leave them in the nursery. If the tears were tremendous, however, we backed off and kept the child with us. It usually took several weeks, or even several months in one case, before the child stayed willingly.

The first few drop-off times, I stayed hidden around a corner and listened to make sure my child was not crying, or quickly stopped crying. If after a few minutes the child was playing contentedly, I went ahead into Mass. If the child was upset, however, I removed him or her from the nursery. This was not necessarily due to some overriding philosophy of child rearing, but more as a courtesy to the meager staff. An inconsolable child demands considerable attention, and can also start a chain reaction among other youngsters. The church nursery works best when the children in it are fairly independent and agreeable.

When our boys were toddlers, the nursery area was staffed by a rotating group of parent volunteers. The nursery space and routine quickly became familiar, but the supervisor was a different person each week. This did not bother our oldest son, but our younger sons, and other children too, sometimes resisted staying with a volunteer they did not recognize. Our parish solved this problem by making the nursery supervisor a paid position and asked one person to be there each week. This is a little more dependable system and also gives the children a familiar face to know. Volunteers work as assistants.

Sending a favorite blankie or bear sometimes helps toddlers feel more secure and eases the separation anxiety, but be careful about allowing a child to bring a favorite book or toy from home. Children learn to think that everything in the nursery is collective property and shareable. It's not fair to the other children to let your child bring in a special toy that is of exclusive use to him/her.

It goes without saying that if our child is sick, we have a

duty to keep the child at home. Unfortunately, I've often seen parents leave children in the nursery who appear to be running a fever, or who are sneezing and coughing. A few days later, of course, our own children are displaying the same symptoms. Another simple courtesy is to offer to take your turn helping, if the nursery relies on a rotating volunteer schedule. You may find it a good way to meet other families with young children, as well as supporting the program. If you do not feel able to volunteer right away, because you have a newborn, for example, let the supervisor know that you will volunteer at a later date.

If you plan to leave the child in the nursery, it's probably best to do so before Mass, rather than bring the toddler to Mass to "see how we get along today," then take him or her to the nursery when inappropriate behavior begins. Our oldest son figured out (before his inexperienced parents did) that if he screamed and threw a tantrum at Mass, he would soon be removed to go play with toys and his buddies. As we tried to extend the duration of his weekly time in Mass, our son escalated his misbehavior accordingly until he could be dismissed to the nursery. Older and wiser, we now offer our three-year-old daughter the choice of nursery or Mass. If she chooses Mass, she must behave accordingly, and the nursery is no longer used as a last-ditch-effort.

When picking up your child after Mass, be prompt, but not early. If you open the door five minutes before Mass is ended, several other young children may start crying, because their parents have not yet returned. Even if it makes for some difficult crowd control, it's best to wait until all the children and parents can be reunited simultaneously.

Finally, be forewarned about relying too heavily upon the nursery. When holidays arrive, in some parishes during the summer months, or when visiting another parish, the nursery may be unavailable to you. A child completely unaccustomed to sitting through Mass can tax everyone's patience. Take the child to Mass with you occasionally, perhaps to a sparsely attended Mass or on a day when you feel rested and patient. In this way, you can begin to teach Mass etiquette and work toward the day when the nursery is not an option.

Split-Mass schedule — Though certainly not an ideal solution, my husband and I resorted to a split-Mass schedule fairly often when our children were in the active pre-nursery stage, between about ten months and eighteen months of age. One spouse attends Mass while the other babysits at home; at a later Mass, the spouses switch roles. Older children can attend with either parent.

Those who choose this option miss out on the sense of family unity and bonding that is possible when both spouses attend Mass together, but each spouse gets to participate in a Mass without major disruption. This can be an oasis of solitude and spiritual renewal in an otherwise loud and chaotic week. Confident that the child is being well supervised at home, the parent can concentrate on the Mass.

If you belong to a large nearby parish that offers a number of Masses each weekend, this may be a fairly painless solution. If you live a longer distance from the parish, or face a more limited Mass schedule, it may be less feasible for you to travel separately. For several months, if my husband and I attended consecutive Masses, we had just enough time to switch roles. As soon as the one attending the earlier Mass pulled in the driveway, the other spouse had to jump into the car and rush to be on time for the later Mass. Like us, you may at times find even this situation preferable to struggling to restrain an uncooperative toddler (or two or three) during Mass.

While temporarily solving the problem of toddler behavior at Mass, be careful about making this a habit for too long, though. Children understandably would rather stay home and play than get dressed up and sit through Mass, especially if one parent is home relaxing with them. (This is especially true if one parent is a non-church goer.) If you expect your children to attend Mass with you regularly as they get older, you will probably need to begin developing the habit at an early age.

Preschoolers

The preschool years are when it is especially important to foster an understanding of church as a special and sacred place. As they outgrow toddlerhood, children's attention span increases, their ability to sit still improves, and they can better understand limits and restrictions that are imposed upon them. Most children at this age have a strong desire to demonstrate that they are "growing up," and display great pride in being able to do things still beyond the reach of those younger than them.

In our family we appealed to these preschool traits by presenting weekly attendance at Mass as a rite of passage. Graduating from the nursery on their fourth birthday, and joining Mom and Dad inside the church "permanently" meant that we parents were confident that the child now possessed the skills necessary for behaving properly at Mass. (Of course, most of these skills were as yet undeveloped, but we tried not to focus on that aspect at the outset.)

As further evidence of this rite of passage, we designated one or two outfits as "church clothes." Once the play room is left behind, we told our children, more care needs to be taken about what we wear to God's house. These clothes were not fancy, but were distinguishable from play clothes, and reserved only for church or another special occasion. "Put on your church clothes," was a meaningful first step in the "Put on your church attitude and behavior" routine.

At this age, we also tried to instill a sense that Mass attendance is obligatory. Especially if the parents are still splitting attendance to minimize frustrations with babies and/or toddlers, it is easy for the older child to want to stay home, too. After the fourth birthday, we established that unless the child was sick, the child came along. Again, we presented this in a positive fashion, although it was not always interpreted as such.

To offset some of the negativity we encountered ("I hate dressing up; I hate sitting still; I hate Sundays!"), we decided to build special privileges and treats into Sunday, as well. This not only mitigated the "pain" of the Mass discipline, but also added to the idea that Sunday is the Lord's Day and therefore worthy of celebration. Sunday became allowance-distribution day and the only free day on the chore chart. We also frequently treated the family to pancake breakfasts, especially after a Mass where few behavior problems had erupted. These simple changes helped shift our children's attitude from "I hate Sundays," to "How many more days until Sunday?" Within this positive context, parents should find it much easier to teach the rudiments of Mass etiquette.

Aside from the basic (and most difficult) task of teaching preschoolers to respect the silence and sanctity of the Mass, this is the age when we can most easily teach the various gestures of the Mass. It may help if you take the child to church at a separate time during the week to practice appropriate behaviors, or model them at home if the church is inconvenient. You can give instructions and the child can ask questions without disrupting the flow of the Mass. Then, come Sunday, he or she can proudly display the newly acquired skills.

As with toddlers, make sure the preschool child has eaten and taken care of bathroom needs before arriving at Mass. Though by this age children usually have good bladder control, it's safer to take a request during Mass seriously than to enforce a wait. As a wise mother of thirteen children writes, "Some children truly can't wait one more minute, and no one wants to meet the new pastor over a mop."[9]

Though many parents seem to arrive at Mass loaded with entertainment gizmos for their preschool child, I'll restate my preference that most or all of those toys remain at home. By this age parents should be able to expect their children to sit quietly and patiently (at least for short periods) at appropriate times, without significant disruption. It does require vigilance and persistence on the part of parents, but it is an investment that will help you and the child, both at Mass and in other situations.

Of course, neither self-discipline nor Mass etiquette are learned overnight. Parents should not expect instant perfection of their child, nor be too severe in their discipline tactics. I was reminded of this fact recently when I read a letter from a man who recalled being left by his parents at the county dump after an Easter Mass because he kept crawling over the pews. Though he was only left alone for a few minutes, he still remembers this frightening punishment forty-three years later.[10] Instead of resorting to such extreme measures, contemporary parents are frequently advised to praise the child's good behavior, thereby reinforcing it, and ignore or downplay the bad. To a large extent, that advice works well with children at Mass, as long as serious misbehavior is not ignored.

Pre-, First Communicants

Ideally, if you work diligently with your children during the preschool years to behave appropriately at Mass, the early elementary years should go quite smoothly. As they begin to approach First Communion age, the emphasis is more on helping them to understand what is happening, rather than keeping them from disrupting the Mass for others.

Occasionally, some horseplay or other inappropriate behavior will still undoubtedly occur, however. How should you handle it? For five- to seven-year-olds, the most effective behavior-modification technique I found was gleaned from a friend whose three children always seemed particularly well-behaved at Mass. Her rule (which became ours) is: For any time spent disrupting Mass, a comparable amount of time must be spent kneeling in prayer immediately after Mass is ended. As all the other parishioners exit after Mass, the offending child and I remain behind to ask God's forgiveness and offer prayers (and check my watch).

Yes, I feel self-conscious and want to rush to the exit, too, especially after an hour spent in behavior battle. It takes fortitude to kneel in the pew, but the prayer is often healing for both of us. Because the goal of the errant child is usually to escape the confines of church, the prolonged delay is a fitting consequence. As veteran parents know, a discipline investment one week may yield a dividend as soon as the next.

This tactic works best if the parent maintains at least loosely the minute-to-minute ratio. Why? If you simply hiss, "O.K., now you've blown it. Stay after for prayer," the child has nothing further to lose and may see no point in reform at that stage of the Mass. Added minutes for further infractions give an ongoing incentive for improvement.

Another big help to us at this age was our local Catholic elementary school. Our children's Mass behavior improved markedly as soon as their teachers began reinforcing what we as parents had been teaching for years. As the children saw some of their friends and teachers attend Mass, modeling appropriate behavior, it became easier for the children to follow that pattern, too. If your parish does not have a school, but has a strong CCD program, you may be able to find similar support there.

Hopefully, by the time our child enrolls in a First Communion preparation class, the basics of good Mass behavior will simply be second nature. Then we can relax and appreciate the privilege of attending Mass together. Coping with children of any age at Mass can be difficult at times, but by helping them become comfortable and confident at Mass we are investing in their spiritual future.

Endnotes

1. *Quam Singulari* decree, quoted in *The Teaching of Christ*, Bishop Donald Wuerl, et al., editors, fourth edition. Our

Sunday Visitor Publishing Division, Huntington, Ind.: 1995, p. 429)

2. *Catechism of the Catholic Church*, English translation. Various publishers: 1994, no. 1345.

3. *Lumen Gentium*, no. 11; quoted in the *Catechism,* no. 2225.

4. *New American Bible*, Matthew 19:14-15; also Mark 10:13-16 and Luke 18:15-17.

5. Cowherd, Kevin, "Life in the Main Scream." *Catholic Parent*, July/August, 1994, pp. 30-31.

6. Galvano, Betty, "Give Credit Where Credit is Due." *Catholic Parent*, September/October, 1995, pp. 18-19.

7. Kuharski, Mary Ann, *Raising Catholic Children.* Our Sunday Visitor Publishing Division, Huntington, Ind.: 1991, pp. 110-11.

8. Ball, Ann, *Catholic Traditions in Crafts*, Our Sunday Visitor Publishing Division, Huntington, Ind.: 1997.

9. Kuharski, p. 110.

10. Reader's comment in "Punishment Won't Make Your Kids Good." *U.S. Catholic*, July, 1996, p. 29.

Chapter Four

Baptism

I n the Catholic tradition, parents usually bring their children to church to be christened within a few months after birth. In a ceremony that is simple yet beautiful, the child is baptized with water and initiated into the Christian faith. This is an important spiritual and social occasion for Catholic families as they celebrate the gift of new life.

Prior to Vatican II, infants were typically rushed to baptism as quickly as possible, often before the mother had even recovered enough from childbirth to attend the ceremony. Current Catholic custom (combined with lower infant mortality rates) encourages parents to baptize their children soon after birth, but also allows them time to participate in a sacramental preparation course and arrange for distant godparents or relatives to attend the ceremony. A typical time-frame is approximately two to four months after birth. Many parishes require parents to attend classes before scheduling a baptism for their child. It is advisable to contact the parish rectory (even before the birth of the baby, if possible) to inquire about the parish's baptism preparation requirements.

If a baby is in danger of death, emergency baptism may be

performed, not only by a priest, but by anyone. Then, if the child survives the crisis, the parents may bring the baby to church later to "supply the ceremonies" in a public celebration.[1] The child will not, however, be "rebaptized," because we receive the sacrament of baptism only once in a lifetime.

While baptism is by no means an exclusively Catholic ritual, there are certain traditions associated with a Catholic baptism that may not be shared by other Christian groups. Understanding these customs can help us better appreciate the ceremony and what part we may play in it. After reading this chapter, I hope you will be able to plan or participate in a baptism for someone close to you, with added confidence and grace.

Background — In the early years of the Church, the sacraments of initiation for new Christians took place as one continuous rite on Holy Saturday. Adult catechumens were typically walked into a river, or later a baptistry, for their baptismal rite, then anointed with a sweet-smelling oil. Often, the initiates were welcomed from the waters by the bishop, as the leader of the local community. He, too, anointed the new Christians with perfumed oil, this time on the forehead in the sign of the cross. Then the newly baptized were dressed in white robes and led to the altar table, to partake of their First Eucharist. A written account preserved from the year A.D. 215 tells us this was the ordinary ritual in Rome at that time.[2]

For adult catechumens, a similar initiation process takes place in the contemporary Church, although baptism by immersion is less common now and the anointing rituals are also more simplified, with the parish priest usually standing in for the bishop. Since the revised rites for adult initiation instituted in 1972, catechumens receive all three sacraments of initiation — baptism, confirmation, and the Eucharist — consecutively, usually on Holy Saturday during ceremonies of the Easter Vigil. For catechumens who were previously baptized in a valid non-Catholic ceremony, only confirmation and Eucharist are conferred.

Baptismal preparation — One way pastors impress upon parents the importance of the role they will play in the spiritual development of their child after baptism is through a sacramental preparation program. These programs typically consist of two, three, or four sessions and may be taught by a priest, a designated layperson, or a team of individuals. Many couples find that the birth of a child gives them an opportunity to reaffirm their personal commitment to the Church and to experience their faith life in a new way. Baptismal preparation programs, especially if run effectively, foster such a reaffirmation and strengthen the family's ties to the parish. Most parishes require parental participation in some type of baptismal preparation class before their first child is baptized. For subsequent baptism requests, the requirement is often waived.

Sometimes, parents wish to have their child baptized in a parish other than their own local church. For example, the extended family may be clustered in a distant location, and the family would like to combine the baptism with a family reunion or holiday celebration. Perhaps the couple moved recently and prefers to celebrate their child's baptism in their previous parish. Under such circumstances, it may be possible to have the child baptized away from home, but the parents need to consult the pastors involved to see what kind of arrangements could be made. Contact your local pastor first, since he should approve any alternate baptism site.

Godparents — Selecting appropriate godparents for Catholic children can be a sensitive issue, since in our society the selection customarily carries social as well as spiritual significance. Unlike some Protestant denominations, the Catholic Church requires that godparents meet some fairly strict criteria in order to qualify as acceptable choices. When many of our closest friends and family members represent different faith traditions, we may feel especially challenged to meet the requirements of the Church and also meet the expectations of those around us.

Exactly what are the qualifications for a Catholic godparent? The *Code of Canon Law* says the godparent must be a confirmed Catholic at least sixteen years of age, who has already received First Eucharist. The godparent must also "lead a life of faith in harmony with the duty he or she is undertaking," and cannot be under a canonical penalty. Parents cannot serve as godparents to their own children.[3]

Only one sponsor is required for baptism, but this person must fulfill all of the canonical requirements for this role. Two (but never more than two) people may be selected as sponsors. If two godparents are chosen, one must be male and the other female.

Our local pastor says that parents frequently put him on the spot by asking two women or two men to serve as godparents, or two women and a man. While this may be customary in some non-Catholic traditions, it simply is not acceptable in the Catholic Church. Please spare yourself (and your family) the embarrassment of asking the priest to bend these rules.

Does this set of restrictions dramatically shrink your pool of potential godparent candidates? A saving grace for those of us faced with these circumstances is that a baptized non-Catholic Christian may take part in the ceremony as a witness, though technically not as a godparent. This enables a close relative or personal friend to fulfill the social role of godparent, and on a certain plane the spiritual role as well, without compromising Catholic teaching. When one side of the family is Catholic and one is not, selecting a baptismal witness can help both sides of the family feel included in such an important occasion.

For purposes of the ceremony, the distinction between godparent and witness need not be made clear. It would be appropriate, however, to make the non-Catholic "godparent" aware from the outset that you are not asking him or her to make a commitment to Catholicism, to help alleviate any unnecessary discomfort.

When Catholics are asked to serve as godparents for a Protestant child, the situation is even more delicate. According to the teachings of the Catholic Church, Catholics are not permitted to be godparents for any child baptized in a non-Catholic religion.[4] In most non-Catholic circles, however, it would be considered deeply offensive to refuse the request to serve as godparent, since it is such a social honor.

Fortunately, the Catholic Church does allow its members to act as "witnesses" at non-Catholic baptisms,[5] thereby enabling us to fulfill the social role of godparent. If you find yourself in this situation, explain to your friend or relative that you will be honored to serve as a "godparent," except that you cannot promise to raise the child in the faith tradition of his or her parents because of your commitment to Catholicism. In many cases, the parents may simply want reassurance that the child will have a Christian example to follow, with no significant attachment to their particular Protestant denomination.

Newly selected godparents (and baptismal witnesses) may be uncertain about what social obligations are inherent in this role. Expectations vary from family to family, but most parents anticipate that the godparents they've selected will attend the baptismal ceremony, bring a gift, and take a special interest in the child as he or she grows to maturity.

Family traditions and personal circumstances will determine the size of our gift, but appropriate baptismal gifts are most often something of lasting value. These may be monetary (e.g. cash or a savings bond), commemorative (e.g. a silver spoon or cup, a photo album, or a treasured book), or religious (e.g. a crucifix or rosary).

According to etiquette maven Charlotte Ford, godparents are the only baptismal guests actually obliged to give a christening present.[6] In most families, though, grandparents and other close relatives traditionally bring the baby baptismal gifts, also. Those who may have already given the child a substantial present at birth are advised to bring an inexpensive but thoughtful gift to the baptism.

Preliminaries

In most American parishes baptisms are scheduled for early Sunday afternoon once or twice per month, although some larger parishes may offer the opportunity for baptism each Sunday. A private ceremony is held in the church for those families and their invited guests — the immediate family, godparents, grandparents, and perhaps a few other family or surrogate-family members.

The presider is usually determined by a rotating schedule, if the parish is large enough to have assistants to the pastor. If you have a preference for a particular person to perform the ceremony, ask to be scheduled on his date if possible. Otherwise, expect to have the designated priest or deacon baptize your child. It is considered discourteous to set the baptismal date, then ask for a particular priest.

Occasionally, the baptism may be administered as part of a regular Sunday Mass. If you would prefer this option, check with your local pastor to see if arrangements could be made to accommodate your request. In smaller parishes, or parishes that include only a few young families, baptism during Mass may be the normal custom. For most parishes, however, it would be cumbersome to incorporate so many baptisms into the weekend Mass schedule.

Parents and other invitees should arrive at the church about fifteen minutes prior to the prearranged baptismal time. Adults and older children typically wear clothing that would be suitable for attending Mass. Since this is an important occasion for the family, it is preferable to err on the side of "too dressy" rather than "too casual."

The infant to be baptized is customarily clothed in white, going back to the tradition of the early Christians, who wore white robes on their baptismal day. In some families, an heirloom christening gown is carefully preserved and passed down to new family members to wear on their baptism day. This type of gown may be worn by babies of either sex, although some parents balk at the idea of seeing their son in a "dress," and select different apparel for the day. In other families, separate christening clothes for boys and for girls may be saved and shared. Consider clothing the baby in a hand-me-down if it is offered to you, as a way of demonstrating the family members' interconnectedness and Christian bond through baptism. The choice of whether to have the child wear something old or new, however, is up to the parents.

If you have any questions about photography limits, it's best to get them answered before the ceremony is ready to begin. Restrictions vary from parish to parish, but paparazzi-style photographers and video enthusiasts obviously detract from the reverence and solemnity of the occasion. It is the parents' responsibility to inform all of their guests about when and where photographs may be taken.

The Ceremony

As part of the baptismal preparation class, parents look at the Rite of Baptism for Children in some detail, so only a few key points of the ceremony will be highlighted here.[7]

One significant change in the baptismal rite (introduced in 1970) is that the parents take a more prominent role, while the ceremonial role of the godparents has diminished. In the ceremony of the past, the godmother typically held the infant and the godparents answered questions that the priest addressed to the child. In the current rite, parents are expected to hold the infant, at least during significant parts of the ceremony. Questions are no longer asked of the child, but are directed to the parents and godparents explicitly.

At the beginning of the baptism rite, the presider will ask three questions of the parents of each child:
1) What name do you give this child?
2) What do you ask of God's Church for (name of child)?
3) Do you clearly understand what you are undertaking?

The question about the child's name is not as straightforward as it may appear. Since the middle ages, Catholics have customarily been given a saint's name at baptism. It was expected that the newly baptized would learn about their patron saint, use the saint's life as a model, and pray to them for guidance and protection.[8] In Catholic countries, it is still a custom to emphasize the feast day of the patron saint — the person's name day — more than a person's birthday.

Today, this naming tradition is largely ignored in America, although the Church still recommends that a saint's name, or a name with Christian significance, be chosen.[9]

The next question is asked of the godparents: Are you ready to help the parents of this child in their duty as Christian parents? After their response, the presider traces a small sign of the cross on the child's forehead and invites the parents and godparents to do the same. One or more Scripture readings, a short homily, and prayers follow.

Then the sacramental rite itself is performed. After some brief preliminaries, the celebrant immerses the child in water three times, or pours water over the head of the child three times, while saying, "I baptize you in the name of the Father, and of the Son, and of the Holy Spirit." Next, the child's head is anointed with chrism, signifying the gift of the Holy Spirit to the newly baptized.[10] Some type of white garment, usually a simple stole, is also placed on the child, as a sign of being clothed with Christ. Then the parents are handed candles lit from the Easter candle, and instructed to "keep the flame of faith alive in their hearts." Brief concluding rites complete the ceremony.

Parents will be given a baptismal certificate and sometimes other mementoes of the occasion, as well. It is important for parents to file this certificate in a place where it can easily be retrieved at a later date. When your child is getting ready to receive his or her First Communion, you will probably be asked to produce this certificate or a copy of it.

One final topic of baptismal protocol needs to be mentioned

— the stipend or stole fee. This is a voluntary but customary offering paid to a priest for the celebration of a sacrament. In some cases, a fixed amount may be suggested by the parish, but more often it is up to the donors' discretion. A typical donation is twenty to fifty dollars, although this varies according to locale and personal circumstances. Cash, or a check made out to the priest personally rather than the parish, is placed in an envelope, then handed discretely to the priest before leaving the church. In some ethnic groups, the stipend duty was traditionally assigned to the godfather, but today the stipend is almost always considered the parents' responsibility.

The priest may refuse such offerings, either as an individual decision or because of diocesan or parish stipulations. Abuses have occurred at times throughout history, and the Church does not want to give anyone the idea that sacraments must be purchased. In some dioceses, stipends and stole fees associated with the administration of sacraments become part of parish income, and the clergy's salary is adjusted accordingly.

Unless you're sure of the local policy, you may want to ask the receptionist or sacramental preparation leader for clarification. If you feel uncomfortable asking, simply give the priest the envelope as described, and trust that he will follow appropriate guidelines.

The Christening Party

After a baptism, the godparents, family, and friends leave the church and gather to celebrate the event. Entertaining guests when a baby (or more than one baby) has so recently joined the household can be tiring and stressful for the new parents. Therefore, the guest list for the christening party should be kept to a minimum, confined typically to those who have attended the baptismal ceremony.

You may certainly invite the priest or other celebrant to the christening party, especially if you are well acquainted. Do not, however, simply extend this invitation at the end of the ceremony. Whether you had given the matter any consideration beforehand or not, such a last-minute invitation gives the appearance of being an afterthought, and may also put the priest in an awkward position. Send a written invitation at least two weeks in advance so that he may plan accordingly and give you a proper response.

The menu should be kept fairly simple, and the burden of entertaining shared if possible. This may be an opportune time to accept a mother's or close friend's gracious invitation to host the party at her place, if the location is not too distant from the church. If the baptismal parents do hold the celebration at home (as is often the practice), considerate local guests may offer to assist with food or other preparations. A buffet luncheon, for example, can be planned to include dishes prepared ahead of time by hosts and by others.

Guests should be understanding, too, if the party (or the appearance of the home) may not be up to the hostess' usual standards. Though I'm not encouraging sloppiness, it is only the exceptional new mother who can pull off a "perfect" party at this time in her life. While a baptism is definitely worthy of celebration, a mother should not be so stressed out over the post-baptismal party that she cannot focus on the important religious ceremony that precedes it, or the child that prompted it.

Allowances should be made for the baby, as well. Though relatives may understandably wish to spend time with the newest family member, most babies are able to join in the baptismal party for only a short time. The child's napping and feeding schedule has probably already been seriously disrupted by the ceremonies. Better to let the child sleep, away from the loving hoard if necessary, than pass a tired and irritable infant from lap to lap. Hopefully, family members will have other opportunities to get to know the child well.

Looking back on my twin sons' baptism party, I remember feeling embarrassed that our new house was not in "showing condition" when the guests arrived, and concerned that houseguests had to help search for certain essentials. I also remember feeling groggy and disoriented, because I had been surviving on so little sleep for several weeks. In retrospect, I think I should have spent less time cleaning, cooking, and apologizing, and more time sleeping!

Since that experience, I've been much more aware of and empathetic to new-parent fatigue. At certain times in our life — even when faced with one-time-only festive occasions — it is important to simplify the peripheral details and focus on the essential. I encourage friends and relatives to respect whatever decisions the new parents make about how they wish to celebrate the occasion, even if those plans may be less elaborate than expected.

Endnotes
1. Stravinskas, Rev. Peter M.J., *The Catholic Answer Book.* Our Sunday Visitor Publishing Division, Huntington, Ind: 1990, p. 89.
2. Described by Greg Dues in *Catholic Customs and Traditions: A Popular Guide.* Twenty-Third Publications, Mystic, Conn.: 1992, p. 153.
3. Paraphrased from Beth Branigan McNamara's *Baptism: The Most Precious Gift*, Our Sunday Visitor Publishing Division, Huntington, Ind.: 1996, p. 18.
4. Foy, Felician and Rose Avato, Editors, *1996 Catholic Almanac.* Our Sunday Visitor Publishing Division, Huntington, Ind.: 1995, p. 224.
5. Ibid.
6. Ford, Charlotte, *Etiquette: Charlotte Ford's Guide to Modern Manners.* Potter, New York: 1988, p. 334.
7. For a more detailed explanation, refer to the McNamara book cited above.
8. Dues, p. 115.
9. See *Catechism*, no. 2165.
10. See *Catechism*, no. 1241.

Chapter Five
First Communion

iven the high regard Catholics hold for the Eucharist, the occasion on which we first receive this sacrament is certain to be marked with special ceremony and anticipation. For those raised in the Catholic tradition, this event customarily takes place during the second grade of elementary school, under the auspices of either the Catholic school or the parish CCD (Confraternity of Christian Doctrine) program. For Catholic children and their families, First Communion is viewed as an important rite of passage and a day that will long be remembered.

Background

Since Pope St. Pius X's decree in 1910 that children who have reached the age of reason (seven years old) could be admitted to the Eucharist,[1] parishes have generally conformed to the practice of celebrating First Communion in the second grade. What is less consistent, and an ongoing source of debate within the Church in some circles, is which other sacraments (if any) should be conferred in conjunction with First Communion.

In most parishes, children prepare for their first reconciliation (confession) prior to First Communion. Preparation used to be simultaneous for these two sacraments (and still may be in some areas), but the current trend is to emphasize the fact that reconciliation and Eucharist are two distinct sacraments. In other parishes, sacramental preparation for reconciliation does not begin until two or more years after the First Eucharist is celebrated. In a few places, children are given the option of receiving either sacrament first.

Religious educators are similarly divided about whether the Rite of Confirmation should precede First Communion or follow it. Standard practice in most American parishes is to confer confirmation at some point during the teen years, but some Church leaders believe the original order of the initiation sacraments should be preserved — baptism, confirmation, First Eucharist. Therefore, in some dioceses, second graders receive both confirmation and First Eucharist on the same day in a combined ceremony.

It is definitely beyond the scope of this book to discuss the relative merits or pitfalls of these various practices. The Church has used several different patterns over the course of the centuries, and the spacing and order of these sacraments is still being discussed, evaluated, and experimented with today. Readers should be aware, however, that this is one area where Catholic practices vary. How the children close to you will experience their First Communion will therefore depend on the policies of the diocese in which they reside.

Sacramental Preparation

Parents are encouraged to take an active role in helping to prepare their child to participate in the sacrament of the Eucharist. Exactly how much parental involvement is required depends on how the program is structured.

For those children attending a Catholic school, a detailed preparation is undoubtedly part of the curriculum, taught during the regular school day. Parents may be asked to review the lessons at home, and/or assist the child with specific projects and homework assignments throughout the year. In addition, parental attendance at one or several sacramental preparation meetings is probably mandatory. The parish's director of religious education or a catechist usually leads these sessions, covering both spiritual and practical considerations for the upcoming First Communion. At this time, the parents are also given the opportunity to ask any questions they may have.

For parents whose children attend a public school or non-Catholic private school, more of the preparation duty will likely rest with the family. Children must be enrolled in the parish religious education program and attend weekly classes, usually after school or sometime during the weekend. The attendance policy preceding the reception of the sacrament may be quite strict, with the responsibility for teaching missed classwork also falling to the parents. CCD parents, too, are typically expected to attend several preparation sessions, at which time both spiritual and practical aspects of the sacrament are discussed.

As with baptism, pastors and Church leaders are concerned that the sacrament not be administered as an isolated event, but offered within a context of active participation in Catholic life. Ideally, parents of First Communicants should be registered members of the parish and already attending Mass there weekly. Both parents need not be Catholic, however, for children to participate in the First Communion program. Families who join the parish during the sacramental preparation period need to consult their local pastor or pastoral staff to find out what requirements and restrictions may apply to their situation.

Preliminaries

First Communion usually takes place as a group ceremony for the entire class, or arranged as two ceremonies if the class is especially large. It is most typically held as a separate Mass on an early Sunday afternoon during spring. The First Communicants usually sit together, and their families and other invited guests fill the rest of the church.

Whom does the child invite? How many close family members you have and where they reside may largely determine your guest list. Family tradition plays a part in the decision, also. Typically, the immediate family (parents and siblings of the First Communicant), grandparents, and godparents, if they have remained close to the child, are included. In addition, aunts, uncles, and cousins may also be invited, especially if you customarily celebrate festive occasions together. If your extended family resides locally and comprises a large group, you may want to invite them to the celebration afterward, but limit those attending the ceremony to a smaller number.

Expect that seating at this event will be limited, and that seating adjacent to the child, if available at all, will probably be restricted to two persons only. If you want to sit in a special place to see your grandchild or godchild more clearly, plan to arrive at least thirty minutes prior to the start of the ceremony, or even earlier in some parishes. While holding seats open for late-arriving family members is occasionally done, this practice is awkward and may cause hard feelings among other guests. Either arrive early, or take your chances on available seating with a later arrival.

In some areas, pastors offer options to this long-standing tradition of a large group ceremony. For example, the First Communion may be incorporated into all the weekend Masses for a particular weekend or two, with a few First Communicants participating in each Mass. In many places, children may also make a First Communion individually as part of a regular Mass, but usually there are special circumstances to warrant this.

It has long been the custom for Catholic girls to wear a white dress and veil on their First Communion day. In some parishes and families, dress can be quite elaborate; in others, simplicity prevails. Catholic boys typically wear dark pants with a white shirt and a tie, a dark suit, or sometimes a white suit. In recent years, some parishes have relaxed these clothing restrictions, although the children are still expected to dress up for the occasion. The school or parish should issue clear guidelines about appropriate clothing for the day, so parents will be able to plan for the child's wardrobe needs well in advance.

I learned through my own experience that novice parents should not necessarily take the printed clothing guidelines at face value, however. When my oldest son was preparing for his First Communion, the distributed guidelines said jackets were optional but not required, so I planned for him to wear dress pants and a shirt, but really gave no thought to a jacket. It was not until about one week before the ceremony that I inadvertently discovered that every other boy in his class would be wearing a jacket and that all of my in-laws were also expecting him to be dressed in a jacket! I then hastily embarked on several nerve-wracking shopping trips, scouring the city until I finally found an appropriate jacket that (just about) fit my son. If you have any doubts about clothing customs for the occasion, ask veteran parents or look at photos of recent First Communion classes at the parish, if they are displayed somewhere.

For this ritual, too, the parish probably has some type of restrictions on photography. Parents should understand and respect the parish policy, whatever it may be, and communicate it to their invited guests. Guests, feel free to bring your cameras, but please inquire about photographic policies if you don't know them, before shooting any photos.

In all likelihood, the parish has an established fee (fifteen dollars in our area) that parents are expected to pay to help cover costs incurred during participation in the First Communion program. This fee is either prepaid sometime in the months preceding the reception of the sacrament, or already included in the enrollment fee paid upon entering the religious education program at the parish. An offering basket may be passed during the Mass, however, and parents of the First Communicants should make a contribution. Considerate guests will also make a small donation when the basket is passed, although it is not required. Even if the First Communion takes place as an individual rather than group ceremony, no stipend is necessary.[2]

The Ceremony

The First Communion ceremony is a Mass, typically following the modifications prescribed for a children's liturgy. Sometimes representatives from the class will participate by reading the Scripture lessons, offering intercessory prayers, and bringing up the gifts. Other times, adults will fulfill those roles, in order not to single out any individual children for special attention, or place them under performance pressure.

When Communion is distributed, the First Communicants typically receive the sacrament first, either with or without their parents, depending on parish custom. Non-Catholic parents, or parents who are under a canonical sanction, may also join their children in the Communion line. As they approach the head of the line, these parents simply indicate to the minister nonverbally that they do not wish to receive the Host. The simplest way to do this is by keeping the head bowed and hands folded, instead of initiating the receptive posture.[3]

Other members of the congregation who do not wish to receive Communion (refer to Chapter Two for Eucharistic restrictions and requirements) may remain in their pews during distribution, or follow the example just described. In this type of ceremony today, many extended-family members and family friends in the congregation are likely to be non-Catholics. By attending the First Communion liturgy, they emphasize their love and support for the child during this important rite of passage, rather than focusing on any theological differences they may have with the family. For this reason, I encourage invited guests to attend if possible, even if they are members of a different faith community.

The First Communion Party

After the ceremony, the children typically pose for group photographs near the altar. Then the parish may hold a short reception in the church for the First Communicants and their guests. When the children leave the church, family and friends gather at the parents' home or some other location to celebrate the event.

Modest family parties have traditionally been the norm, but as with other children's parties, the scale and expense of entertainment, especially in some communities, have been escalating. In some families, the First Communion party may come close to a Bar Mitvah or small wedding in lavishness. In most families, however, a buffet dinner or cake and ice cream reception suffices. Do not feel compelled to match your neighbors' entertainment style, but simply plan a tasteful celebration that you feel is appropriate to the occasion.

Anyone invited to attend a First Communion celebration should bring or send a gift for the child. Traditional gifts include money or savings bonds, and religious items such as rosaries, religious books, or medals. Your local Catholic bookstore or religious goods store, if you have one, should carry a supply of appropriate items in varying costs.[4]

Non-Catholic guests need not purchase something foreign to their beliefs. An item such as a rosary is best given by someone who venerates Mary and sees the rosary as a legitimate spiritual aid, rather than by someone who has never used one. On the other hand, Protestants should take care not to give any gift that could be considered overtly Protestant in nature either. For example, some popular books by certain Evangelical authors are viewed as nondenominational by Protestants, but may be seen differently by Catholics. Consult with a knowledgeable clerk or check with the child's parents for gift ideas if you're unsure.

A monetary gift presented in an appropriate card, perhaps with an attractive bookmark or other token gift, would be welcomed by any child and his or her family. In some communities with a small Catholic population, secular card shops may not have any First Communion cards on display. Sometimes less-frequently requested cards are stored in a non-display area, though, so ask a clerk for assistance before giving up your search. If you cannot find an appropriate card, or do not care to search for one, a personal note written on an all-occasion card would be equally acceptable.

By this age, children should be taught to receive gifts graciously and thank the donors politely, also. If by some chance the child opens gifts outside the parents' presence (which can happen sometimes if the parents are busy preparing a meal, or if guests are arriving and leaving at different times), some other adult should help make sure the child keeps cards and the corresponding gifts together. Written thank-you notes from the child, sent the following week if possible, are a nice gesture to those who have brought gifts to the First Communion party. Written notes, or at least a phone call, are expected for gifts sent via mail.

The First Communion rite and its celebration provide a good opportunity to help your growing child develop both spiritually and socially. Wise parents will not allow the child to neglect the social duties that accompany this important step in the process of Catholic initiation.

Endnotes

1. *Quam Singulari* decree, quoted in *The Teaching of Christ*, Bishop Donald Wuerl, et al., editors, fourth edition. Our Sunday Visitor Publishing Division, Huntington, Ind.: 1995, p. 429.
2. Stole fees or stipends are customarily offered to the clergy only at baptisms, weddings, and funerals.

3. Other recognized gestures include a raised index finger across the lips, or arms across the chest in the shape of an X. The latter is a posture more commonly used with children, however, and the raised finger may not be familiar to many ministers.

4. If no religious good stores are convenient locally, several good mail order supply sources are available. Two examples are: Abbey Press, St. Meinrad Archabbey, St. Meinrad, IN 47577; and The Printery House, Conception Abbey, Conception, MO 64433.

Chapter Six

Confirmation

The Sacrament of Confirmation continues the Christian initiation process begun at baptism, drawing the baptized more fully into the life of the Church. Through the laying on of hands and an anointing with a perfumed oil called chrism, the bishop "imparts the gift of the Holy Spirit that completes the grace of baptism."[1]

In the Eastern churches this rite is still conferred immediately after baptism, and is called "Chrismation," meaning to anoint with chrism. (Eucharist, too, is then customarily offered to all new Christians in the Eastern Church, regardless of the age of the recipient.) In the Latin rite of the Catholic Church, however, the sacrament is conferred some years after baptism (except in the case of newly baptized adults), and is seen as "confirming" the baptismal anointing.

Of the sacraments of initiation, confirmation is the one that varies the most widely in how and when it is celebrated. In the United States, the age at which Catholic children are confirmed ranges all the way from seven to eighteen, and the customs surrounding the sacrament are being changed in many areas, also. Therefore, it is difficult to discuss a "typical" confirmation ceremony and its corresponding protocol with much precision. While the universal Church shares certain common understandings about confirmation, the timing and administration of the sacrament depend on parish and diocesan preferences, and sometimes personal circumstances, also.

Historical Background

Confirmation was first recognized as a distinct rite by Pope Cornelius (r. 251-253), although it was not known by the name "confirmation" until the mid-fifth century.[2] As the Church grew and infant baptism became more prevalent, bishops found it increasingly difficult to anoint each new initiate at their baptism. Therefore, baptism and confirmation soon became separated. The parish priest typically baptized newborns shortly after birth, and the bishop would anoint all the newly baptized on his next visit to the parish.

While the basic anointing ritual has not changed all that much since its inception, the customary confirmation age has changed numerous times over the years. For many centuries in the early Church, it was expected that confirmation would follow soon after baptism, usually occurring before the child reached the age of two. Then, sometime after the thirteenth century, the confirmation age began moving upward — to seven, then twelve, then fourteen. American bishops, as part of the post-Vatican II reforms in 1972, redefined the proper age for confirmation as between the ages of ten and twelve. The most recent trend is to defer confirmation until the later teen years, when its significance for mature Christian living becomes more evident.[3]

Sacramental Preparation

Like First Communion, the preparation program for the Sacrament of Confirmation is structured and supervised by either the Catholic school or the parish CCD organization. For those attending Catholic schools, confirmation often occurs just a few weeks prior to graduation from the eighth grade, thus serving as a culminating point of their years of religious training in elementary school. For students in CCD programs, official preparation usually begins at least one year prior to confirmation, as a part of the weekly catechism classes. CCD attendance policies may be strict, and confirmands may also be required to pass an exam that tests their knowledge of Catholic teachings and practices.

The prevailing attitude is to emphasize confirmation as a sacrament of Christian maturity. By personally reaffirming the faith professed by his or her parents at baptism, the confirmand demonstrates a commitment to live a Christian life. After confirmation, the confirmands are considered "adults" in the eyes of the Church.

Once in a while, an adolescent may express concern that he or she does not feel ready to make this affirmation. Parents in this situation should be willing to listen to the concerns and perhaps help put things in perspective by sharing some of their own faith history. If the problem persists, a private talk with the pastor may also help answer the teen's questions or doubts. Ultimately, though, the child should freely choose to participate in the confirmation, or postpone it until a later date.[4]

Sacramental preparation for confirmation focuses not only on developing a deeper understanding of the faith, but also includes some type of Christian service project. Projects may be personal and close to home, such as choosing to babysit for a younger sibling or helping a neighbor with yardwork. More often, however, the service project involves a group of confirmands volunteering time at a soup kitchen, collecting needed items for a homeless shelter, or some other effort that reaches beyond the daily routine. Since modern teens experience so much social pressure contrary to Christian ideals, this is a particularly important time to emphasize Church teachings and to help channel teen energy in a positive direction.

The Church requires a sponsor for the person being confirmed, following the same guidelines as those given for a Catholic godparent. The sponsor must be a practicing Catholic at least sixteen years of age, who has received the sacraments of confirmation and Eucharist, and is free from canonical sanction. Preferably the baptismal sponsor, or one of the baptismal sponsors, serves as the confirmation sponsor, also.[5] If circumstances have changed, however, and the baptismal godparent is no longer an appropriate choice, another sponsor may be chosen. Parents may not serve as sponsors for their own children. Unlike at baptism, non-Catholics are not asked to participate as sponsors or witnesses for the confirmand, although they may certainly be included in the larger celebration of the sacrament.

Another tradition which echoes baptismal symbolism is the selection of a confirmation name. Once a familiar part of this rite of passage, the naming custom is followed less frequently today. In some confirmation classes, however, studying about the lives of the saints and selecting a saint's name as a personal choice is a significant part of sacramental preparation. While some confirmands may take this as a challenge to come up with the most unusual choice, others find courage and solace in aligning themselves with one of these models of Christian virtue.

Preliminaries

A group ceremony for the class is often scheduled to coincide with a visit to the parish by the diocesan bishop, although some parishes have switched to small group or individual confirmations presided over by the parish priest. Springtime remains the most popular time for this ceremony, but confirmation may take place at any time throughout the year.

Confirmation clothing is no longer distinctive in most places. Girls select modest dresses and boys typically wear a blazer and dress slacks. Several months before the ceremony, the school or religious education leadership should provide parents and confirmands with clear guidelines about what they consider appropriate and inappropriate attire for the occasion. Practical thinking nowadays is that confirmation clothing should be something that may be worn again for other occasions, rather than a one-time-only choice.

Seating guidelines should also be offered, especially if this is a large group ceremony. Confirmands are usually seated together, either with or without their parents, and family members and guests fill the remainder of the church. As with First Communion, those who wish to sit on the aisle or near the front should plan to arrive at least thirty minutes prior to the start of the ceremony. For individual or small group confirmations incorporated into a weekend Mass, a small seating section is typically reserved for the confirmands and their immediate families. Whatever the arrangement, parents of the confirmands should communicate to their invited guests when to arrive and where to look for seating.

Parish photography restrictions may be familiar to you and your family by now, if your child has been baptized and has received First Communion in the same parish. In this case, a simple reminder to your guests should suffice. If you have moved to a new parish, though, be sure to ask about their policy on photographs. Since rules vary from place to place, you cannot assume that what was acceptable at one parish will be equally acceptable at the next.

As with First Communion, a fixed fee may be established by the parish to cover incidental expenses associated with the sacrament's preparation and administration. This should be prepaid, either as a separate fee or as part of the religious education enrollment fee. A personal stipend is not necessary for this ceremony, but an offering basket may be passed during the Mass. As with other occasions, guests may put a donation in the basket, but are not required to do so.

The Ceremony

The confirmation ceremony from earlier times emphasized the idea that the sacrament gave strength and fortitude to the candidates, so that they could defend their faith and fight as a "soldier of Christ" if necessary. A rigorous question and answer session where candidates were grilled about their faith and challenged to come up with memorized answers was a major part of this ritual. In another unique feature of the old rite, the bishop lightly tapped or slapped each recipient on the cheek. This gesture was introduced during medieval times and remained in the confirmation rite until the early part of this century. Of course, the bishop's "slap" became part of adolescent lore, and older children often teased the younger ones about this "painful" aspect of the ceremony.

Today's confirmation ceremony (revised in 1971) assumes a different attitude, although it still emphasizes the strengthening of the baptized by the Holy Spirit. Confirmation is usually conferred in the context of a Mass (after the Gospel reading), but can be administered as a private ceremony also.

In either case, the Liturgy of Confirmation begins with the confirmands renewing their baptismal promises and making a profession of faith. The bishop then extends his hands over the candidates, and invokes the outpouring of the Holy Spirit.[6] Confirmation thus shares a strong connection to Pentecost, the day when the apostles received the gifts of the Holy Spirit.

In the essential Rite of Confirmation, the bishop or priest lays his hands upon the confirmand and anoints him or her on the forehead, saying, "Be sealed with the gift of the Holy Spirit," or "Receive the seal of the gift of the Holy Spirit." A shared sign of peace completes the ritual.

The Celebration Party

The confirmation party resembles the First Communion party, a festive gathering of family and close friends to commemorate the occasion. Unless circumstances have changed considerably, the people you invited to the child's First Communion party are the same guests you would invite to the confirmation celebration — grandparents, godparents or sponsor, and close family and surrogate family members with whom you typically celebrate. The party is most often held at the parents' home, but may also take place at another location if desired.

Guests are expected to bring a gift, with the value depending upon family custom and how close you are to the child. Appropriate choices are religious books or symbols, jewelry, a pen and pencil set, savings bonds, or money, or often a combination of money and a small gift. Invited guests who are unable to attend the ceremony should send a gift to the confirmand, also.

Teens should be able to greet guests warmly, help offer refreshments, and accept gifts graciously. Hopefully by this time, it will be second nature for the adolescent to express thanks to the donor as the gift is opened. Written thank-you notes sent the following week, are a courteous gesture, but not mandatory. For any gifts sent via mail, thank you notes or at least a telephone thanks are expected. Just as the confirmand is assuming more personal responsibility for his or her spiritual life, he or she should now be able to assume more social responsibilities personally as well.

Adult Initiation

Adults are usually brought into the Church today in a combined initiation rite administered during the Easter Vigil. Typically, they prepare and study for at least a year prior to the date, as part of a group of catechumens in the RCIA (Rite of

Christian Initiation for Adults) program. The initiation ceremony confers baptism, confirmation, and First Communion consecutively.

Adults who have been baptized in a Protestant ceremony and wish to join the Catholic Church usually do not need to participate in the full catechumenate program. Some instruction and formation must be offered, however, and these adults are typically initiated as part of the RCIA group, also. In some cases, a private initiation ceremony may be held at other times of the year with only the sponsor and perhaps the immediate family attending. Check with your pastor or parish secretary to find out what the options and requirements may be for your specific situation.

The parish often hosts a small reception for the group following the Vigil, including sponsors and immediate family members, also. Sponsors should give the newly baptized a gift with religious significance, but it need not be costly. Since adult baptism and confirmation are seen more as personal rather than social events, any further celebration is most often confined to the immediate family, or shared with other RCIA participants.

Sometimes adults who were raised as Catholics somehow miss out on the opportunity to receive the Sacrament of Confirmation as a child, perhaps as the result of frequent family relocations. For adults in this situation, bishops in most areas hold confirmation ceremonies several times per year at the local cathedral. Check with your parish pastor if you wish to participate in such a ceremony to find out about preparation requirements. Since confirmation is only conferred once, however, you will probably need to verify that you have not received the sacrament at an earlier date.

At whatever age we receive them, the sacraments of initiation help join us with the millions of Christians who have participated in these sacraments before us. Ideally, preparation, ritual, and celebration combine to make these ceremonies not only grace-filled spiritual events, but also beautiful and memorable occasions for the participants and their loved ones.

Endnotes

1. *Catechism of the Catholic Church*, English translation. Various publishers: 1993, no. 1288.
2. Bunson, Matthew, *Our Sunday Visitor's Encyclopedia of Catholic History.* Our Sunday Visitor Publishing Division, Huntington, Ind.: 1995, p. 221.
3. Described by Greg Dues in *Catholic Customs and Traditions: A Popular Guide.* Twenty-Third Publications, Mystic, Conn.: 1992, p. 154.
4. The booklet *How to Talk to Your Child About Confirmation* by William Odell (Our Sunday Visitor Publishing Division: 1993) may help parents approach the subject and clarify some of the issues for their teen.
5. Foy, Felician and Rose Avato, Editors, *1996 Catholic Almanac.* Our Sunday Visitor Publishing Division, Huntington, Ind.: 1995, p. 225.
6. See *Catechism*, nos. 1298-99.

Chapter Seven
Reconciliation

hat used to be commonly referred to as "going to confession" or the Sacrament of Penance is now customarily referred to as the Sacrament of Reconciliation. As the name change implies, the sacrament has undergone a change in emphasis following Vatican II. As one author succinctly explains, "Today the sacrament . . . is more about patching things up than about punishment."[1] For many centuries private confession took place near the altar of the church. Then, in the late sixteenth century, the confessional box (a confessor's chair boxed in by screens) was designed by St. Charles Borromeo to allow the penitents total anonymity. Until Vatican II, the confessional box remained the ordinary site for receiving the Sacrament of Penance.

In the new rite, reconciliation rooms have replaced the confessional box as the typical place for conferring the sacrament, although the traditional confessionals have been retained as an option for those who are more comfortable with them. In the reconciliation room, the penitent has the option of kneeling anonymously behind a screen or sitting directly across from the priest to talk with him face-to-face. As Father Leonard Foley has noted, the face-to-face method requires "trust, humility, and courage,"[2] but for many the experience is healthy and liberating.

Reconciliation is one sacrament where content really takes precedence over form. Even if we freeze under the tension of the moment and forget all protocol or rehearsed words, the priest will guide us through the ritual. A simple and heartfelt admission of guilt and a sincere desire to change a pattern of bad habits or poor choices is all we really need voice.

Background

Penance and absolution practices within Catholicism have changed and evolved over the centuries, probably undergoing more modifications than any other sacrament. According to research, penances in the early Church were harsh and often public and sometimes lasted for years or even a lifetime. Less serious sins did not require public penitence, but were believed to be forgiven by the traditional penitential practices of prayer, fasting, and almsgiving.

By the seventh or eighth century (perhaps earlier, according to some researchers), a practice of private confession which had developed within Irish monasteries spread to mainland Europe. People embraced the idea, and the practice took hold. Assigned penances gradually became less strict and less public, and people began to take advantage of the sacrament more frequently. By the year 1215, the Church required people to make an annual private confession to a priest, thereby officially sanctioning what had begun as an unofficial form of penance.

Over the centuries, a theology regarding mortal sins versus venial sins also began to develop. Mortal sins (those previously requiring public penitence) were said to merit eternal punishment if not forgiven during one's lifetime. Venial sins were described as not serious enough to affect our eternal salvation, but still requiring some retribution either before or after death.

Eventually, the Church and its members became involved in a kind of penance economy. People could go to confession, perform some type of penance, and thereby erase part or even all of their temporal debt to God (a debt understood to be payable by time in Purgatory if not settled in this lifetime). Partial or full remissions of temporal punishment called indulgences, either could be obtained for oneself or credited to the soul of a specific person who had died. Unfortunately, during the middle ages these indulgences came to be associated with financial donations, a practice which helped fund the Church and support individual priests, but ultimately served as a catalyst for the Protestant Reformation in the sixteenth century.

For those of us steeped in Protestant history and theology during our formative years, images of these medieval abuses may still reflexively come to mind whenever we hear the term indulgence. Current Catholic teaching regarding indulgences reflects a more contemporary (and sophisticated) theology, however. The Church still encourages special acts of charity and devotion as a means of remitting temporal punishment in the afterlife, but it no longer makes any attempts to attribute exact amounts of time in a debit or credit column.[3]

Preliminaries

The revised ritual for the Sacrament of Reconciliation, first issued in 1974, gives two different forms for celebrating the sacrament: individual confession and a communal penance service, which is a group ceremony with individual private confessions following it. A third form — general absolution without individual confession — is only for extraordinary circumstances of "grave necessity" and normally not an option for most of us.

Let's take a closer look at these two common forms of celebrating the Sacrament of Reconciliation to see what we can expect, and what may be expected of us.

Individual Penance Ceremony

The individual form of the sacrament is often offered at most parishes on Saturday afternoons, with the time specified in the parish bulletin or elsewhere. Priests may be available at other times as well, through private appointment. If you cannot find the time posted, or if Saturday afternoon does not work into your schedule, contact the parish office to verify times and availability. In the "old days" the Saturday afternoon lines apparently were long, but in most places the wait is not lengthy today.

The Sacrament of Reconciliation is composed of four elements: contrition, confession, absolution, and penance. In order for the sacrament to be valid, we must first be genuinely sorry for the sin, take responsibility for it, and have a firm intention not to repeat the same mistake. Prior to meeting with the priest, we are expected to examine our conscience and identify times when we have personally failed to live up to God's moral teachings.

When it is our turn to enter the room, we either sit in the available chair across from the priest or kneel behind the screen. Then, as the confessor greets us, we make the sign of the cross. He may (or may not) read a brief Scripture lesson that reminds us of the importance of repentance.

We then tell the priest about recent occasions of sin (and older sins also if they have not been confessed previously) and perhaps some of the circumstances surrounding them. In the past, the penitent initiated the confession with the prescribed formula, "Bless me Father, for I have sinned. . . ," then recited a prepared list of sins and the estimated number of occasions for each. This format has given way to a less formal structure today. The priest listens, and may offer some advice or encouragement. The one truth about confession that even non-Catholics seem to know (from the movies or novels perhaps) is that the priest is bound to keep secret whatever he hears in private confession.

The priest will then impose a penance that corresponds with the gravity and nature of the sins committed. According to the *Catechism of the Catholic Church*, this penance "may consist of prayer, an offering, works of mercy, service of neighbor, voluntary self-denial, sacrifices, and above all patient acceptance of the cross we must bear."[4] Penitents then traditionally recite an act of contrition, a prayer that expresses to God the sorrow we feel and a willingness to avoid sin in the future. If we do not have this prayer memorized, we may voice this contrition spontaneously, in our own words.

At the close of the ritual, the confessor extends his hand or places his hands on our head, and recites the words of absolution: "God, the Father of mercies, through the death and resurrection of his Son has reconciled the world to himself and sent the Holy Spirit among us for the forgiveness of sins; through the ministry of the Church may God give you pardon and peace, and I absolve you from your sins in the name of the Father, and of the Son, and of the Holy Spirit."[5] Penitents answer, "Amen." A prayer of praise may or may not be included before the priest dismisses us, and we exit the room.

Communal Penance

Often scheduled during the preparatory seasons of Advent and Lent, the communal penance service is becoming a seasonal ritual for many Catholics. It features song, prayer, Scripture reading, preaching, and a guided examination of conscience, followed by the individual sharing of the Sacrament of Reconciliation just described. By joining in the sacrament as an assembly, the communal aspects of sin and reconciliation are emphasized, along with the private aspect.

Courtesies to keep in mind at a communal service are primarily concerned with maintaining the solemnity of the occasion and expediting the process. While priests from neighboring parishes often assist the parish pastor(s), and several reconciliation rooms are typically made available, a line of penitents will still likely form for each priest.

Those most experienced at this type of service sometimes choose a seat near an exit, then bolt for the nearest priest as soon as the words of dismissal are spoken. While this practice helps ensure a spot at the front of the line, reverent Catholics restrict their sprinting to the track (or airport), and adopt a more dignified pace when proceeding to the confessional. Those less familiar with the ritual will likely move less decidedly, and may be startled to suddenly find themselves at the end of a line of twenty or thirty people.

Whatever our position, we can make use of our waiting time to examine our conscience further, to reflect upon the Stations of the Cross or other art in the church, to pray, or to simply wait quietly. It definitely detracts from the dignity of the sacrament when people around us chat casually, as if they were in line to buy tickets to a ball game.

At the same time, we should not completely lose awareness of the people around us, either. I am thinking of one occasion where I was waiting in a long line of penitents after a service. A few spaces in front of me stood a young couple with two toddlers. (For some reason, babysitting was made available during the communal service, but not extended to parents afterward.) I doubt if any of us in line that evening appreciated the wait. We were probably all anxious to take our turn and head home after a long day, but I am certain the wait was more difficult for these parents of two toddlers whose bedtime had already passed.

During the forty minutes we were waiting in line, the parents took turns wandering with the boys, carrying them, cajoling, etc. I had to admire the fortitude these parents showed by continuing to wait their turn, even as their young children began increasingly to lose patience with the wait. As the line entered the anteroom of the reconciliation chapel, there were about ten people still in line ahead of this couple. At this point, the boys started climbing over chairs, tossing hymnals, and wrestling. The rambunctious behavior and whining grew louder, and the children were clearly distracting not only the parents, but all of us who were waiting.

I kept thinking to myself, "Surely, one of these ten people will offer this couple his own place in line or allow them to jump ahead." Being a novice at this sacrament, I hesitated to suggest the idea to someone else, and my own place was behind the young parents. Not one person, however, offered this couple the chance to go ahead. They dutifully waited (and the rest of us dutifully endured) until their turn naturally arrived.

For all of us, though, I think it would have been a courtesy to allow this couple the opportunity to step to the head of the line. If you find yourselves in similar circumstances where someone behind you in line is obviously having a hardship by waiting (the elderly or frail, someone on crutches, or in the last months of pregnancy, perhaps) consider offering to trade spots, even if it adds a few extra minutes to your own wait. Think of it as a bonus penance.

Parents of young children who do not wish to be caught in such a situation should try to leave the children in someone else's care. Parish leaders may wish to suggest that if babysitting time after the penance service is limited, parents whose children are in the nursery be permitted to avail themselves of the sacrament first.

The communal penance service does not replace the individual penance form, but is an alternate way of celebrating the sacrament. Communal penance services can be a deeply satisfying way to experience the Sacrament of Reconciliation, especially if we adopt a patient and penitent attitude about time that may be spent waiting our turn. An evening spent in prayer, reflection, and devotion is an appropriate context for this sacrament.

First Reconciliation

In most places, children who are born Catholic participate in their first reconciliation prior to their First Communion, usually in second grade or about age seven. In other parishes, first reconciliation is delayed until age nine or ten (see page 84). Preparation is handled through either the Catholic school or CCD program of the parish.

Often, the immediate family is invited to join the child at the first reconciliation service, a communal penance service with private confession afterward. Depending on local custom, the parents and older siblings either follow the child in making a private confession themselves or remain seated in the pew while the child alone makes a confession. The emphasis during the preparation stage and the service itself will be more on God's forgiving love than on the child's sins.[6]

The parish may provide some cookies and juice after the sacrament, but otherwise this event is celebrated quietly. The immediate family lends their support and encouragement to the child making a first confession, but gifts and parties such as those that accompany the child's First Communion are not appropriate for this occasion.

Adults preparing to join the Catholic Church make their first reconciliation along with other RCIA students or individually with their pastor prior to receiving their confirmation and First Eucharist. (Those who will receive the Sacrament of Baptism upon entering the Catholic Church do not have their first reconciliation until after confirmation and Eucharist, as baptism cleanses them from sin.) Those who were not raised in the Catholic tradition may initially find this sacrament intimidating and difficult. When pastors are aware that someone is participating in the sacrament for the first time, though, they are usually sensitive to apprehension and generous with their time and encouragement. Though converts may never feel as comfortable with the idea as cradle Catholics, we often come to appreciate the unique qualities of this gift, also.

Hearing God's words of forgiveness spoken to us personally can help us feel comforted about the past and more confident about the future. Being able to leave our mistakes behind us and start afresh is a true spiritual gift.

Endnotes

1. Meara, Mary Jane Frances Cavolina, et al., *Still Catholic After All These Years.* Doubleday, New York: 1993, p. 13.
2. Foley, Leonard, O.F.M., "Why Confess My Sins?" (Catholic Update series). St. Anthony Messenger Press: 1984.
3. For an explanation of current teaching regarding indulgences, refer to the *Catechism*, nos. 1471-79. The *1996 Catholic Almanac* (Our Sunday Visitor Publishing Division: 1995) also gives a detailed explanation of how to obtain an indulgence on pages 314-15.
4. *Catechism*, no. 1460.
5. Order of Penance 46, formula of absolution. Quoted in the *Catechism*, no. 1449.
6. Neumann, Lori, *In the Lord's Peace.* Our Sunday Visitor Publishing Division, Huntington, Ind.: 1996, p. 97.

Chapter Eight

Anointing of the Sick

he sacrament known for centuries as Extreme Unction or Last Rites was renamed following Vatican II, and is now commonly referred to as Anointing of the Sick. Although it is no longer reserved exclusively for those *"in extremis"* as the older term implied, the sacrament is still one we generally receive only once, or a very few times in our lifetime. This anointing rite can bring comfort and grace to the dying, and can also bring God's healing graces to the seriously sick or aged who are not in immediate danger of death.

Because Anointing of the Sick is such a uniquely Catholic sacrament and because of the post-Vatican II revisions, many of us may not know quite how or when to avail ourselves of this sacrament. Most of us have probably had little personal contact with the ritual, yet any one of us could find ourselves facing a decision about whether or not to request the sacrament if an accident or serious illness were suddenly to occur. Hopefully, the information in this chapter will give you some additional insight into the purpose and protocol of this sacrament, so that you may prepare yourself or a loved one to receive the sacrament when the need arises.

Background

The Letter of James (5:14-15) describes clearly a healing ritual within the early Church: "If one of you is ill, he should send for the elders of the church, and they must anoint him with oil in the name of the Lord and pray over him. The prayer of faith will save the sick man and the Lord will raise him up again; and if he has committed any sins, he will be forgiven" (RSV).

The Catholic Church has maintained this apostolic practice of anointing the sick ever since, although it has been carried out in different ways over the years. In the early centuries of the Church, the blessed oil was regarded as a sacramental substance through which God could effect physical cures, and apparently used much like a medicinal ointment or salve.[1] Later, as the emphasis shifted from physical to spiritual healing, the ritual was reserved more and more exclusively to the critically ill. Then, in the mid-1960s, the second Vatican Council reexamined this sacrament and decided to restore some of the more ancient practices, albeit with a more sophisticated understanding of theology and medicine. A revised rite was published in 1973.

Now, when we anoint the sick, we pray that God will give whatever healing the person entrusted to His care most needs. The blessing over the oil for anointing expresses this beautifully, as the priest asks God to "make this oil a remedy for all who are anointed with it; heal them in body, in soul, and in spirit, and deliver them from every affliction."[2]

Currently, the Catholic Church has several different forms for celebrating the sacrament of Anointing of the Sick, depending upon circumstances. It may be held in a communal setting, a semi-private setting, or a private one. Usually this sacrament is celebrated in conjunction with the sacraments of penance and the Eucharist. (Penance precedes it and the Eucharist follows the anointing.) When it is a probable last anointing of someone who is critically ill or dying, the priest administers the Eucharist as Viaticum, food for the passage through death to eternal life.

Timing and Preparation

For many generations, one of the most difficult questions for caregivers and family members of a critically ill Catholic has been, "When should I call the priest?" Because of the "Last Rites" connotation, loved ones were reluctant to summon the priest, although they wanted to be certain that a priest could arrive prior to death. This hesitancy frequently meant that the sacrament was delayed until the sick person had lapsed into unconsciousness or was so debilitated that he or she was unaware of the ritual taking place.

Modern reforms have eased this dilemma a bit, since the timing is no longer viewed as being so critical. People are encouraged to avail themselves of the Sacrament of Anointing while they can still appreciate on a conscious level the sacrament's comfort and derive strength from it. It is also acceptable to receive the sacrament more than once if health conditions change. According to the guidelines in *Pastoral Care of the Sick*, "the sacrament may be repeated if the sick person recovers after being anointed and then again falls ill or if during the same illness the person's condition becomes more serious."[3] This expanded availability often allows the decisions about "When? Where?" and "With whom?" to rest more in the hands of the patient, rather than with caregivers or family.

Getting back to that difficult question, just when should we call the priest to administer the sacrament? The *Constitution on Sacred Liturgy* says, "As soon as one of the faithful begins to be in danger of death from sickness or from old age, the appropriate time for him to receive this sacrament has already arrived."[4] In practice, opportune times are before major surgery, at the onset of treatment for some serious health problem, or when an elderly person begins to weaken, even though no serious illness has been diagnosed. Children who are in danger of death may receive the sacrament also, if they have reached the age of reason (seven years).

Though much of the responsibility now rests with each Catholic personally, relatives and friends may still need to assist the sick in calling the priest and helping loved ones prepare to receive the sacrament. While it is undeniably painful to anticipate death, the revised Anointing of the Sick rituals can help bring comfort and grace when they are most needed. Since it is not necessarily associated with immediately impending death, the sacrament may be somewhat easier to embrace. Anyone who broaches this subject must certainly exercise sensitivity and tact, however.

One experienced pastor suggests we talk to a loved one who is ill or very old about the real significance of the anointing.[5] After such conversational groundwork, we can then offer to contact the priest. I think the same advice can be applied in reverse, also. Those who are ill or old may wish to talk at least briefly with a loved one about what the sacrament signifies before asking him or her to contact the priest or join the ceremony. Especially if the friend or relative is unfamiliar with Catholic practices or the changes in emphasis since Vatican II, such a request could be unnecessarily frightening if unexplained.

Special Circumstances

What should we do if we are a devout Catholic and a sick loved one is a "lapsed Catholic"? Even if Catholicism is an unpopular topic, it is best to talk frankly and sincerely with the patient about our concern for his or her spiritual welfare. Sometimes well-meaning relatives arrange a "surprise" visit from the priest for someone who has been away from the sacraments for years. The sick person may have no intention of welcoming either the priest or the idea of confession, and everyone is put in an awkward position. If we are unsuccessful in talking with our loved one about the sacrament but would like a priest to visit anyway, we must at minimum warn the priest that the patient may not receive him warmly.[6]

What if we are a devout Catholic and one of our loved ones is a critically ill non-Catholic? The Sacrament of Anointing can be administered to any baptized Christian, although the Catholic Church is the only Christian church which regards Anointing of the Sick as a real sacrament. The best idea would be to talk about the sacrament and its meaning sometime before a medical emergency or serious illness occurs. Then we would have a better understanding of the person's preferences and desires in a critical situation. In general, though, spouses should respect the faith tradition of the sick person and contact the appropriate clergy, although a priest may certainly be invited to pray with the sick and the grieving. Priests and considerate family members, however, will be reluctant to do anything that could give the impression of imposing Catholicism upon the sick.

What if someone becomes suddenly debilitated and cannot personally make any decisions about the sacrament? The Church teaches that people who are unconscious or who have lost the ability to reason may be anointed, "if, as Christian believers, they would have asked for it were they in control of their faculties."[7] Catholics typically put great faith in this sacrament and may be fearful of dying without a final priestly blessing. For this reason, many wear medals or carry cards that read: "I am a Catholic. In case of accident, please notify a priest."

Medical personnel and family members should honor this important request, even if they do not understand it. It would be an added hardship to Catholic family members to learn that a Catholic was not offered this opportunity because a non-Catholic spouse or insensitive medical team did not consider it necessary.

If the spouse or other close relative is non-Catholic and has made no effort to contact a priest, a Catholic friend or family member may gently offer to initiate the contact.

If the person is already dead by the time the priest arrives, the priest will not administer the Sacrament of Anointing. He will instead offer prayers, asking God for forgiveness and salvation for the one who has departed, and comfort for the mourners.

Let's look more specifically now at what we can expect when participating in an anointing ceremony.

The Communal Ceremony

Some parishes offer communal anointing ceremonies for the sick and infirm, as part of a Mass. These may be held in the church, or sometimes at a local nursing home as well. Those who wish to avail themselves of such a service but need assistance can request an assistant from the parish, if no relative or friend can attend. If we learn about an upcoming communal Anointing of the Sick that could be beneficial to someone close to us, it may be appropriate to invite that person to the service.

It also may be interesting to attend one of these services even though we or our loved ones are not in immediate need of the sacrament. While not participating in the anointing, we can offer prayers and support for those in need, and see for ourselves what the ceremony involves.

The Mass begins in the usual manner, including Scripture readings and perhaps sacred music and song. The anointing ceremony takes place after the homily. Prayers are first offered for those who will be anointed and those who care for them. Then the sick come to the altar, where the priest lays his hands on the head of each person to be anointed. After praying over the oil, the priest then makes the sign of the cross with the blessed oil on each sick person's forehead, saying: "Through this holy anointing may the Lord in his love and mercy help you with the grace of the Holy Spirit." All respond: "Amen."

Next, the priest anoints the palms of the sick ones' hands with the sign of the cross, and says: "May the Lord who frees you from sin save you and raise you up." All again respond: "Amen." At the conclusion of the ritual, all return to their seats and the Mass proceeds with the Liturgy of the Eucharist. [8]

The Private Ceremony

Many pre-Vatican II Catholics will remember the crucifix that slid open to reveal a vial of holy water and small candles, a fixture in nearly every Catholic household. These items were to be used by a priest during an Anointing of the Sick ceremony. Nowadays though, if a priest is summoned to the home for a medical emergency, it is no longer customary to meet him at the door with a lighted candle. It is helpful, however, to have a clean and uncluttered table or nightstand near the patient, and a fresh glass of water nearby.[9] In a hospital room, it is helpful to anticipate the same simple requirements. The priest will bring everything else that is needed.

In a hospital room or at home, the sick person, and possibly his or her family also, may be encouraged to personalize the ceremony by choosing the Scripture readings and prayers. Often the family is present and participates in the ceremony, unless the patient prefers a private ritual. The family will always be asked to leave the room during the Sacrament of Penance, if the patient wishes to make a confession prior to receiving the anointing. Ideally, no haste will be involved and the rite can be comforting and meaningful to everyone present.

The rite begins with the sign of the cross. As all present are sprinkled or signed with holy water, the minister asks us to "call to mind our baptism. . . ." The Scripture readings, adapted to the condition of the sick person, follow. Then, a litany is prayed, with all present responding, "Lord, have mercy," to each petition.[10] The priest lays his hands on the sick person, then gives thanks over the oil. He then anoints the forehead and hands of the sick person. A prayer follows, then all join in the Lord's Prayer. If the sick person is to receive Communion, then others present may also receive the sacrament. The anointing concludes with a blessing for the sick person and all present.

Even though this may be an emotional time for family members, please remember to thank the priest for coming, and show him to the door. It is not customary to offer any kind of stipend for this service, however. The priest will probably ask to be kept informed of the patient's progress and will reassure the patient and family of the parish's prayers.

Anointing of the Sick requires little else in the way of etiquette or protocol. The most important thing for us to remember is to take advantage of the sacrament — or help others to take advantage of the sacrament — before it is too late.

Endnotes

1. Dues, Greg, *Catholic Customs and Traditions: A Popular Guide.* Twenty-Third Publications, Mystic, Conn.: 1992 (Revised Edition), p. 165.
2. *Pastoral Care of the Sick*, no. 123, quoted by Thomas Richstatter, O.F.M., in "Anointing the Sick," *Catholic Update* Series. St. Anthony Messenger Press, Cincinnati, Oh.: 1995.
3. Quoted in *Catholic Household Blessings and Prayers* by the Bishops' Committee on the Liturgy, National Conference of Catholic Bishops. United States Catholic Conference, Washington, D.C.: 1988, p. 262.
4. *Constitution on Sacred Liturgy*, 73. Quoted in *The Teaching of Christ*, edited by Bishop Donald W. Wuerl, et al., fourth edition. Our Sunday Visitor Publishing Division, Huntington, Ind.: 1995, p. 436.
5. Kenny, John J., *Now That You Are a Catholic.* Paulist Press, Mahwah, N.J.: 1986, p.42.
6. Adapted from Kenny, p. 41.
7. *The Rite of Anointing*, quoted by Wuerl, p. 436.

8. Adapted from an outline in Richstatter's "Anointing the Sick."
9. Kenny, p. 40.
10. *Pastoral Care of the Sick*, quoted in *Catholic Household Blessings and Prayers,* p. 257, 264.

Chapter Nine
Holy Orders

oly Orders is the sacrament of ordination in the Catholic Church, whereby candidates are officially commissioned to carry out the ministry of the Church. Like marriage, Holy Orders is considered a sacrament of consecration, marking the beginning of a lifelong commitment. Therefore, like a wedding, it is a significant occasion in the life of the candidate and his family. If you receive an invitation to attend some or all of the festivities connected with a Holy Orders ceremony, consider it a rare opportunity that should not be missed.

In this chapter, as we look at some of the ceremonial details and protocol associated with the Sacrament of Holy Orders, our focus will be from the guests' perspective. Traditionally, each diocese or religious community provides its candidates and their immediate families with the specifics of how, where, and when things will be done in conjunction with a particular ordination ceremony, so there is no point in trying to collect that information here. (Of necessity, the resulting compilation would be either too general to be of much use anyway, or likely to be inaccurate for some specific situations.) Instead, the information in this chapter is designed for those who may be invited to attend a Holy Orders celebration, but are outside the direct information loop. We will give an overview of some of the highlights of an ordination weekend, and some of the social customs commonly associated with them.

In addition, since an ordination is an occasion where we are likely to meet or be introduced to numerous members of the clergy, this chapter seems an opportune place to discuss some of the appropriate etiquette when meeting various ecclesiastical representatives. Some of the formalities and deference shown to the clergy in the past have been relaxed in recent years, but cradle Catholics, as well as non-Catholics and newcomers to Catholicism, may be uncertain about how to greet or address ranking clergy members. To help you, we will outline some of the different positions within the Church hierarchy and what forms of address and protocol are expected.

First, however, let's look briefly at the history of the Holy Orders sacrament and some of the key concepts associated with it.

Background

Key to our understanding of the Catholic priesthood is the concept of apostolic succession. Throughout the world, Catholic priests have all been ordained by the laying on of hands, receiving a spiritual power conferred from generation to generation only by bishops who have themselves been ordained in the same fashion. Through the Sacrament of Holy Orders, bishops transfer the spiritual duties entrusted first to the apostles by Christ to subsequent generations of priests.

Catholics take this tradition seriously, and it is undeniably one of the major obstacles to greater Christian unity. Catholic clergy trace their ancestry to Christ as the ultimate priest, to the apostles, and then in unbroken succession to the bishops and priests of today. In Catholic eyes, only those who have been ordained through the Sacrament of Holy Orders share this direct lineage.

What this means is that Catholic priests are not interchangeable with Protestant clergy, but are a distinct and separate entity. The sacramental duties entrusted to them cannot, therefore, be delegated to anyone outside the priesthood. Two other prominent characteristics also differentiate the Catholic clergy from many of their Protestant counterparts, namely that Catholic priests are celibate and exclusively male.

Categories of Orders

Although Holy Orders is a once-in-a-lifetime sacrament, there are three different sacramental orders within the sacrament — deacon, priest, and bishop. Each successively higher level confers additional sacramental powers and responsibilities. Thus, a person can actually participate in a Holy Orders ceremony up to three times in his lifetime.

Deacons — In pre-Vatican II days, candidates for the priesthood had to advance through seven different degrees, each with its own ceremony. This process was dramatically simplified, however, as part of the Vatican II reforms. Now, men officially enter the clerical state when they are ordained as "transitional deacons" prior to their final ordination as priests.

This is a significant occasion, but since it is only a transitional step on the path to the priesthood, it is usually celebrated on a smaller scale than the final ordination. Family members and closest friends will likely be invited to witness the ceremony and congratulate the new deacon, as he moves into the final phase of preparation for priestly ordination. Other friends will want to send a congratulatory card or note to the candidate on reaching this important milestone, but are not as likely to be included in the celebration. For those attending the diaconate ceremony, modest gifts to the candidate are appropriate, unless he is part of a religious community that disavows personal property. Gifts are generally not required from the wider ranks of well-wishers. While deacons cannot celebrate Mass, they can be invaluable assistants to the priest. Some typical duties include administering baptism, blessing marriages, reading Scripture lessons and giving homilies at Mass, officiating at funerals and burial services, and bringing Viaticum to the dying.[1] Not all men ordained as deacons are on the path to the priesthood, however. Since 1967, with the restoration of the permanent diaconate, men who cannot or do not wish to be priests may be ordained as permanent deacons. For example, qualified married men may be ordained as deacons if they have the consent of their wives. These men perform the same functions as transitional deacons, but usually on a part-time basis, maintaining their former roles in business and family.

The permanent diaconate is a growing and vital group within the Catholic Church today,[2] but it is still a new enough category to cause occasional misunderstanding when distinctions between deacons and priests are not clear. At my daughter's baptism, for example, the presiding deacon startled some of my Catholic in-laws as well as my own non-Catholic relatives when he began reminiscing fondly about his own children and their baptism days. It was not until after the ceremony was over that my husband and I were able to reassure our guests that this "radical priest" was in reality a married man who had been recently ordained as a permanent deacon.

Because the ordination of a man to the permanent diaconate is not a transitional step, but a final one, he may want to invite many of his family and friends to join him in the celebration. How simple or elaborate the reception may be depends upon the personal circumstances of the new deacon and his family, and the policies of the diocese he will be serving. Also, since this is a relatively new variation on the more familiar transitional diaconate ceremony, the traditions and celebrations surrounding this event are still evolving. If you receive an invitation to a permanent diaconate ceremony, check with the candidate's parents, spouse, or pastor to see what type of gift might be most appropriate for this occasion.

Permanent deacons are never addressed as "Father," but may be called "Deacon (last name)" or "Deacon (first name)." Transitional deacons are properly referred to as "Reverend Mr. (last name)" rather than "Deacon (last name)." If in doubt, ask how the new deacon would like to be addressed.

Priests — The ceremony most commonly associated with the Sacrament of Holy Orders is the elevation of a candidate from deacon to priest. This is a momentous occasion, and one which the young man and his family will certainly want to celebrate with relatives, friends, and supporters. Much like a wedding day, the ordination day is anticipated for months, and is often an emotional time for parents and siblings and close friends, as well as for the candidate himself.

The ceremony itself is often an impressive, awe-inspiring Mass, an occasion where the full pageantry of the Catholic Church is proudly displayed. The service is long (at least one-and-one-half hours or more) and laden with symbolism and time-honored rituals. Usually, the ordination takes place at a cathedral, although in some dioceses the ceremony may be performed at the candidate's home parish instead. In addition to the presiding bishop, it is customary to include other invited clerical guests in parts of the ceremony, also.

In smaller dioceses, only one priest may be ordained in a given year. When this happens, the ordination ceremony and the accompanying reception may be planned individually, with input from the candidate's family as well as the seminary and local diocese. Candidates who are ordained at their home parish may similarly experience some flexibility in planning the ceremony. More typically, however, dates and many of the details for ordination are determined institutionally, because classmates who will be serving in the same diocese are ordained in a group ceremony. This also means that each candidate must strictly limit the number of guests he invites to the ordination, because they will be sharing seating space with guests of all the other candidates, also.

If you are fortunate enough to be invited to a priestly ordination ceremony, plan to allow plenty of time for parking and seating. In some places, it may be necessary to arrive up to an hour ahead of time in order to find relatively good seats. This is probably an occasion to leave the children in someone else's care, too, unless they have been specifically asked to come and you're sure they can behave appropriately throughout this long service.

Guests should wear clothing that is dressy but comfortable. Generally, clothing appropriate to a midday wedding would be equally acceptable for this occasion, although a stronger emphasis on modest and conservative choices does apply.

Bulletins or program booklets are usually distributed by ushers to help guide guests through the various parts of the ceremony and Mass. Not many in the congregation will be familiar with much of this liturgy, but the participatory parts should be fairly easy to follow. When in doubt about whether to stand, sit, or kneel, try to follow the cue of those in the front pews, as they are most likely to hear what the presider is saying and also may be the most prepared about what to expect in this service.

Be careful, though, about whose behavior you're mimicking, so you do not make the same mistake I did at a recent ordination. After getting confused about the actual starting time for the service (we were traveling between time zones), my husband and I arrived late and stood in the aisle for about one-half hour. Then, an usher led us to a spot on the side of the sanctuary where there was one vacant seat immediately behind a large group of priests. Pillars blocked my view of most of the congregation, but I had a great view of the sanctuary, and I suppose I became quite caught up in the beauty and emotion of the event. When all those in front of me stood, I stood, too, until my husband elbowed me. Then, I looked around to realize that the only people standing were all the priests — and me. Needless to say, I quickly sat down, and took my cues from the non-clerical guests seated near me for the rest of the service.

Following the ceremony, guests usually gather nearby, perhaps on the grounds of the cathedral or in an adjacent building, to greet the newly ordained priest(s) and the other guests. Light refreshments are typically served and the atmosphere is festive and celebratory. In some places, this reception is sponsored by the diocese or parish; in others the family must assume responsibility for any gathering after the ordination ceremony. The new priest is now correctly addressed as "Father (last name)" or "Father (first name)."

One interesting custom in some communities is to have the new priest autograph the bulletin as a souvenir of the day. I'm not sure what the history behind this tradition is, but it was popular with the many guests at the last ordination I attended. The newly ordained seemed to expect this request, and complied whenever asked.

First Mass

A second significant event associated with ordination is the new priest's first Mass. Typically, this is scheduled for the day after the ordination ceremony, and takes place in the priest's home parish. Those who may have been unable to be included on the guest list for the ordination ceremony are often invited to share in this Mass, along with more intimate family and friends.

Seating resembles that of a wedding, in which family members are seated up front, while parishioners and other guests take the pews toward the back of the church. When it is time for Communion to be distributed, ushers will direct the priest's parents to receive from their son first, then encourage other close family members to follow. Similarly, at the end of Mass, when all proceed to the front of the church to receive an individual blessing from the new priest, the same processional order will apply. Non-Catholics in attendance will not be able to receive Communion, but are welcome to come forward for the blessing at the end of the Mass, if they wish.

After the First Mass, an informal reception will likely take place in the parish hall. A more formal reception and meal for invited guests may take place later in the day, as well. This may be at the parents' home, at the church, or at a reception hall or restaurant, depending on the entertaining preferences of the parents and priest, and possibly the preferences of the diocese or religious community. (Some Church officials limit the size and lavishness of the celebration, to avoid detracting from the solemnity or importance of the Mass itself.) In some places, the diocese or parish may host part of the celebration, but more often it is the priest's family who arrange and host the accompanying festivities.

Invitations to any of the more formal social events associated with the ordination weekend will be sent out several weeks in advance, asking guests to R.S.V.P. by a certain date. It should go without saying that if you receive such an invitation, you should by all means respond as asked. Unfortunately, many people today take these requests too lightly, and either fail to respond at all or change their mind arbitrarily after responding, whether in the affirmative or the negative.

Please realize (if you do not already) that the host(s) must arrange for food, drink, and space for an anticipated number of guests, and will be strongly inconvenienced if the anticipated number proves to be too few or too many. Caterers require a final guest count at least forty-eight hours in advance, and most bill the hosts based on that count. In other words, if we say that we will attend but then decide at the last minute we'd rather just stay home, our hosts will be charged for our unserved meal anyway (something that even the most easygoing or wealthy hosts are likely to resent). On the other hand, those guests who fail to respond at all to a printed invitation are usually counted in the "no" column. When many of these people show up at the dinner anyway (as I'm told happens with alarming frequency), the hosts may be thrown into a panic as they scramble to secure additional meals and seating to accommodate the unexpected extras.

The reasons people display this type of cavalier attitude toward invitations and their senders I'll leave others to debate. (Schedule overloading, indecisiveness, too many business/organization-sponsored "invitations" that deliberately blur the distinction between customer and guest, a general decline in manners. . . ?) Whatever the root causes, none of these problems validly excuses guests from the social responsibility of responding to an extended invitation. Guests are not obligated to accept an invitation, but they are obligated to answer it. Hopefully, readers of this book are more considerate of hosts, and respond clearly and well in advance to an ordination invitation, or any other invitation, when they receive it.

Gifts

Anyone who receives an invitation to a priestly ordination should probably give or send a gift to the new priest, whether able to attend the ceremonies or not. As with other occasions, the size of the gift will depend upon how close we are to the candidate and our own personal circumstances. It is preferable to send or deliver any gift in advance of the occasion, but we may also bring it with us to the reception, if necessary. Gifts in envelopes are easier to handle at the reception than gifts in boxes, however.

What type of gifts are appropriate for the newly ordained? This will vary considerably according to the individual, his interests, and his circumstances. Most priests are just graduating from student life and will appreciate some personal or household essentials. Others who enter the priesthood later in life may have already acquired many of those items. Some men would like to get gifts that enhance or support one of their favorite hobbies or pastimes, while others prefer more practical gifts.

In a few metropolitan areas, Catholic book/religious goods stores offer an ordination gift registry similar to a bridal gift registry. Candidates visit the store and mark their preferences, then guests select a gift from among the listed items. This is one way to minimize the unnecessary duplication of clerical gifts that sometimes happens at ordination celebrations, but it is not a widely available option at this time.

Cash is a universally popular ordination gift. Whether used to defray the cost of entertaining, to purchase a first car, or to buy some needed reference books, the gift will certainly be appreciated. If you feel uncomfortable with a cash gift, contact the candidate's parents or sibling, and ask for an alternate gift suggestion. A gift certificate may be another good option.

For those being ordained in religious communities, check with the parents, pastor, or other knowledgeable family member before purchasing or sending any gift. Some orders are especially strict in their gift policies, and may require any gift to be given to the community or a charity, rather than to an individual priest.

Anniversaries

For future reference, at the end of the ordination weekend, note the date on your calendar. Just as married couples like to commemorate the anniversary of their wedding date each year, priests appreciate congratulatory notes on the anniversary of their ordination to the priesthood. Perhaps years from now, you, your children, or your grandchildren may be invited to celebrate the silver jubilee (twenty-fifth anniversary) or golden jubilee (fiftieth anniversary) of this ordination, also.

Bishops

Bishops are elevated from within the ranks of priest, and only a relatively small number are chosen to receive this Holy Orders ceremony. Ordination as bishop is considered the fullness of the Sacrament of Holy Orders.[3] After ordination, bishops are entrusted with the authority to ordain priests and are usually designated the administrative and pastoral leader for a particular diocese.

A bishop's ordination is often a social event for the whole diocese, as well as for the man's family and personal friends. Taking place in the diocese where the new bishop will serve, it is an occasion for him to meet some of the people he will be serving and an opportunity for them to meet him, also. Invitations are typically sent to representatives of various local Catholic organizations, parishes, and businesses, as well as all of the Catholic clergy in the vicinity. It is an honor to be included in this number, and invited guests should make every effort to attend if possible.

Like the priestly ordination, a bishop's ordination is an elaborate and lengthy ceremony involving numerous priests and invited clerical participants, the cathedral choir or other diocesan musicians, and many traditional rituals. Expect that the ceremony and the subsequent reception may stretch over the better part of a day. Here again, only exceptionally mature children will be able to behave appropriately throughout this entire event, so they are not likely to be invited.

Following the ceremony, a reception organized by the diocese will probably be held nearby. A receiving line may be set up to allow visitors the opportunity to greet and congratulate the new bishop. Although in pre-Vatican II days it was customary to greet a bishop by kneeling to kiss his ring, this gesture is rarely seen in contemporary America. Similarly, bishops used to be commonly addressed as "Your Excellency," but this, too, is a fading tradition. Today, a simple handshake, and "Congratulations, Bishop (last name)", or "Welcome to our community, Bishop (last name)" should suffice. Bishops are almost never addressed as "Bishop (first name)."

Except for close friends and family, gifts are not expected to be given on this occasion. If we wish to commemorate the day, however, we are always free to give a donation to the cathedral or to a charity or parish within the new bishop's diocese.

Forms of Address for Other Clergy and Religious

At the post-ordination reception, or on other occasions, we may be introduced or want to introduce ourselves to members of the Catholic hierarchy. Many of the outward signs of deference from an earlier era have all but disappeared from popular usage, but it is still important to show respect for their office and calling by referring to them politely. Here are some of the most common Catholic titles, and their customary form of spoken and written address.

Sisters are female members of a religious order. At one time a distinction was made between the terms "sister" and "nun," but today the words are used interchangeably. (Traditionally, "nun" referred to those women in cloistered or contemplative orders, while "sister" was used for women whose primary work took place outside the convent, such as teachers or nurses.) Modern nuns may or may not wear a distinctive habit, depending on the rules of their order and personal preference.

In former times, when women formally professed their vows (chastity, obedience, and poverty), only the immediate family was permitted to attend the ceremony. It was considered a solemn rather than social event, and gifts to the newly initiated were not permitted.[4] Times have changed, however, and today family members and friends may be invited to the ceremony, and a more celebratory atmosphere may prevail. Check with the woman's parents or her community to find out whether a gift would be considered appropriate for the situation, since protocol varies widely among the various religious orders.

In written address or in a formal introduction, use "Sister (name)," followed by the name of her religious order (e.g. Sister Debra Brown, of the Missionaries of Charity). Find out in advance whenever possible whether the sister uses both a first and last name, or whether she more frequently uses just one name. In the past it was common to abandon one's given name and take a new name upon entering religious life. Today, however, sisters usually retain their given name.

When writing, the order name may be abbreviated to initials. Be careful, though, because the accepted initials sometimes are derived from a language other than English, and may not be obvious. Use the abbreviation only when you are certain it is correct.[5] In formal terms, the order initials are not strictly required in correspondence with sisters, but are commonly used.

When speaking to a nun, address her as "Sister (name)", or simply as "Sister." Calling her by her first name, without the title "Sister," would be considered rude or disrespectful in almost all situations.

Brothers are male members of a religious community who have taken vows of chastity, obedience, and poverty, but are not priests. They may perform duties similar to those of deacons, although they often teach, work in the medical field, or serve in some other line of work, also.

Each community has its own particular emphasis and policies, so the rituals accompanying the candidates' formal entry into religious life also differs from place to place. In the past, gifts were not considered appropriate for the occasion, but today they may be expected and welcome. Check with someone close to the candidate or his order who can best inform you.

Introduce a brother as "Brother (name), of the (Religious Order)" (for example, "Brother Paul Smith, of the Franciscan Brothers of the Holy Cross"). In greeting, address him directly as "Brother (name)" or simply "Brother."

Whenever referring in print to someone in a religious community, the initials of the order are generally added to his name, although in the strictest sense these initials are mandatory only for the priests and abbots in religious communities.

Again, check the *Catholic Almanac* or a similar source if you're unsure of the precise abbreviation.

As with sisters, custom varies with regard to name, so ask or listen carefully when introduced to learn whether the brother commonly goes by a single name or uses a surname as well. Some men retain use of their given name after entering religious life, while others select a new name to indicate a new life. The term "monk," incidentally, is a term used to refer to men — either brothers or priests — in contemplative life. You may still hear it used occasionally when referring to members of certain orders.

Deacons and their spoken forms of address have been described previously. According to the *Official Catholic Directory*,[6] in writing a transitional deacon should be referred to as "Reverend Mr. (full name)," while a permanent deacon should be addressed more simply as "Mr. (full name)." Other sources suggest the use of "Deacon (full name)" when writing to a permanent deacon and "Reverend Mr. (full name)" when writing or referring to a transitional deacon.

Religious priests are those who have received Holy Orders but are also members of a religious order or congregation. Recent statistics show that about one-third of all priests in the United States fall into this category.[7] In writing, they should be referred to as "Reverend (full name)," followed by the initials of their order.

When greeting a religious priest (that still seems like a redundant phrase), call him "Father (last name)" or "Father (first name)," if he prefers it, or simply "Father." In more casual introductions, you may use the nickname of his community (e.g., "This is Father Frank Jones, a Paulist"). In more formal introductions, however, the official name of the group should be used (for example, "Our guest speaker this evening will be Father Frank Jones, of the Society of Missionary Priests of St. Paul the Apostle").

Diocesan priests, also sometimes called (oddly enough) secular priests, comprise the majority of priests in the United

States (about two-thirds). Their obedience is to their local bishop, rather than to a leader of a religious community. Diocesan priests primarily serve as parish pastors.

Follow the same guidelines in speech and address as those given for a religious priest, except that no initials or order name need be given. When speaking directly call him "Father (last name)," or "Father (first name)" if he prefers it, or simply "Father." In writing, a priest is referred to as "Reverend (full name)," or in a formal salutation as "Dear Reverend Father."

Monsignor (literally, "my lord") is an honorary title designating those singled out for papal recognition for their service to the Church. Those priests receiving this distinction are called "Monsignor (last name)." In writing, the correct address is "Reverend Monsignor (full name)."

An **abbot** is the head of a monastery. Originally, abbots were all heads of monasteries in the Order of St. Benedict, which dates back to the fifth century A.D. As the monasteries were so important to the Church for so long, abbots came to have a very special place. In some cases they even vest as bishops, although they are priests. They are addressed as "Father Abbot." In writing they are addressed as "Right Reverend (last name)."

Bishops and **archbishops** are typically administrative heads of dioceses and archdioceses, respectively. Currently, thirty-three metropolitan areas in the United States are considered archdioceses. In speaking, the correct title followed by last name should be acceptable in most situations (for example, "Archbishop Smith" or "Bishop Jones"). Previously, people addressed bishops and archbishops as "Your Excellency," but this is rarely used today, at least in America.

In writing, a two-line form of address is used. On the first, write "The Most Reverend (full name)," and underneath include, "Bishop (or Archbishop) of the Diocese (or Archdiocese) of. . . ."

Cardinals are sometimes called the "Princes of the Church," and it is from within their ranks that each new pope is chosen. Cardinals are selected by the pope and are inducted into the College of Cardinals in appropriate ceremonies. Worldwide, there are only one-hundred-fifty-two cardinals; in the United States just a dozen.

Cardinals are often also archbishops, but the title of cardinal takes precedence. In speech, the older custom of "Your Eminence" is still used, even though at times these men are also addressed more simply as "Cardinal (last name)." In writing, a cardinal is addressed as, "His Eminence Cardinal (full name)." If he is also an archbishop, the next line would read "Archbishop of . . . ." A custom originating in the seventeenth century places the title between the first and last name (for example, James Cardinal Johnson). In the most formal situations, this is still considered correct, although the more standard order of title — first name, last name — is used in most secular and religious news publications.

The **Pope** has several titles, but in writing he is most simply referred to as "His Holiness Pope (name)." Those fortunate enough to meet the pope personally should address him as "Your Holiness," or "Holy Father." In news-style writing, the honorific is generally omitted.

If in doubt as to how to address or greet a visiting cleric, check with your local pastor, the local diocesan offices, or the editor of your local diocesan newspaper in advance. For additional assistance in writing to members of the ecclesiastical hierarchy or preparing a publication of some kind that includes references to them, consult *The Official Catholic Directory*, the "Ecclesiastical Titles" entry in *Our Sunday Visitor's Catholic Encyclopedia,* or the *Catholic News Service's Stylebook on Religion*.[8] Additional information regarding ecclesiastical entertaining and protocol and Vatican protocol can be found in an extensive book by James-Charles Noonan, Jr., entitled *The Church Visible*.[9]

Though dealing with representatives of the Catholic hierarchy can be intimidating at times, these few simple guidelines should help you navigate these situations with additional poise. Since usage of titles and courtesies still varies with age, ethnicity, and milieu, some latitude is recognized and accepted in most all situations.

Endnotes

1. From Vatican II's *Dogmatic Constitution on the Church* (No. 29), quoted in *Our Sunday Visitor's 1996 Catholic Almanac*, Felician Foy, O.F.M. and Rose Avato, editors. Our Sunday Visitor Publishing Division, Huntington, Ind.: 1995, p. 229.
2. In 1995, there were 11,371 permanent deacons serving in the United States and its protectorates. (Statistic from *The Official Catholic Directory*, quoted in the *1996 Catholic Almanac*, p. 435.)
3. *Lumen Gentium* 21, section 2, quoted in the *Catechism of the Catholic Church*, no. 1557.
4. Fenner, Kay Toy, *American Catholic Etiquette*. The Newman Press, Westminster, Md.: 1962, p. 53.
5. The *Catholic Almanac* is one good source for verifying initials of religious communities.
6. *The Official Catholic Directory*, P.J. Kenedy and Sons, Wilmette, Ill.: 1995, p. A-16.
7. Statistic from *The Official Catholic Directory*, as quoted in the *1996 Catholic Almanac*, p. 435.
8. *Catholic News Service Stylebook on Religion*. Catholic News Service, Washington, D.C.: 1990.
9. Noonan, James-Charles Jr., *The Church Visible: The Ceremonial Life and Protocol of the Roman Catholic Church*. Viking, New York: 1996.

Chapter Ten

Marriage

wedding is one of the most significant and beautiful occasions in our lives, yet it also is an occasion that carries the highest social expectations and etiquette demands. No matter how well-matched the bride and groom may be, this event still involves two families who may have very different ideas about what such a ceremony and the accompanying celebration(s) should entail. At times, the bride and other principals may feel as if they are crossing an etiquette mine field, where any misstep could set off an emotional explosion.

To complicate matters further, the Catholic Church holds several unique views on the Sacrament of Matrimony, views that are often at odds with those of the culture at large. Thus, Catholic families attending or planning a wedding frequently face additional etiquette concerns that stem from a collision between the mainstream American culture and fundamental Catholic teachings. When the bride or groom is Catholic but the intended spouse is non-Catholic, or when one (or both) of the partners has been married previously, the potential for trampling on an unforeseen "etiquette landmine" is even greater.

In this chapter, we will examine some of these difficult etiquette issues, along with some of the simpler ones. Without being able to resolve theological conflicts for you, or give definitive answers about your specific situation, I can point out areas of frequent concern and offer some etiquette guidelines for negotiating these trouble spots. Respecting Catholic teachings, while also remaining sensitive to the attitudes and feelings of others around us, may sometimes challenge us to search for creative solutions.

Dozens of reliable etiquette books have been written about planning wedding ceremonies and receptions, so I will let other guides help you decide who pays for what, what constitutes formal vs. semi-formal wedding attire, or what to serve at the reception. Similarly, any good general etiquette book should be able to offer advice on appropriate wedding gifts, or the basic social duties of a wedding attendant or guest. What I will try to focus on here are those wedding elements peculiar to Catholicism, that may not be covered adequately by popular etiquette authors.

Background

The Catholic Church teaches that marriage, like Holy Orders, is a sacrament of consecration, entailing a lifelong commitment. According to Catholic marriage law, "A valid and consummated marriage of baptized persons cannot be dissolved by any human authority or any cause other than the death of one of the persons."[1] This firm Church teaching on the permanence of marriage accounts for many of the policies and practices that we may encounter relating to weddings. Despite the sometimes casual way that contemporary Americans treat marriage (and divorce), the Catholic Church maintains that entering into marriage is a serious, lifetime commitment, one that requires careful consideration and preparation.

A second basic teaching that overrides many Catholic marital rules is that "the Catholic Church claims jurisdiction over its members in matters pertaining to marriage." [2] This issue especially comes into play when one of the marriage partners is Catholic and the other is not (a so-called "mixed marriage"). Unless the couple seeks special permission and fulfills certain conditions, the Catholic Church will not regard as valid any wedding ceremonies involving Catholics which take place before non-Catholic ministers or civil authorities. (In fact, prior to 1966, Catholics who celebrated marriage before a non-Catholic minister were considered excommunicated.)

As we look in more detail at some of the protocol and requirements for participating in a valid Catholic marriage, you will soon see how these two basic teachings influence many of our attitudes and procedures.

Sacramental Preparation

Though policy varies somewhat among dioceses, an engaged couple is usually expected to contact the pastor of the Catholic church where they plan to be wed at least six months before their anticipated wedding date. Customarily, the couple is married at the bride's home parish, or in some cases the groom's parish. Occasionally, a wedding may be celebrated in a different Catholic church (the parents' home parish perhaps), but this requires permission from the bride and/or groom's pastor as well as the pastor of the other church. Merely "shopping around" for the most photogenic church in which to hold the ceremony is strongly discouraged.

When the bride is non-Catholic, it still may be permissible to hold the wedding in her home church. For such a wedding to be recognized by the Catholic Church, however, the couple must obtain special permission through the Catholic partner's pastor. The couple should contact the groom's pastor at least six months before the anticipated date to find out what steps are required, and to determine whether this could be a workable option for them. Then, the bride should talk with her own pastor to see if he or she is agreeable to the plan, also. Usually a priest attends the ceremony, and offers prayer and a blessing for the couple, while the host pastor acts as the primary officiant.

Only a few dates are strictly prohibited as Catholic marriage days, namely Holy Thursday, Good Friday, and Holy Saturday. The entire season of Lent is viewed by most Catholics as a rather inappropriate time for wedding festivities, though, because of the seasonal emphasis on penitence. If the date you've tentatively selected falls within Lent, you may want to choose an alternative date instead. In contrast, May, June, and October are especially popular months for weddings, so those dates tend to fill up quickly, especially in large parishes. You may need to reserve the Church for one of those months as much as a year in advance, or else remain flexible in regard to the time of day for your ceremony.

Whether just one or both of the prospective marriage partners are Catholic, almost every parish asks that the couple participate in some type of diocesan-sponsored or parish-sponsored premarital counseling program. Formats and times vary (half-day, one-day, full weekend, or several weekly sessions) but all include basic instruction about Catholic teaching on marriage. In addition, leaders focus on key issues in a marriage relationship, such as child rearing, finances, and decision making, encouraging couples to begin a dialogue on these topics before serious conflicts arise.

Catholic weddings also include a few consent formalities not normally associated with non-Catholic weddings. The prospective bride and groom will be asked to give the pastor copies of baptismal certificates, First Communion, and confirmation certificates when applicable. If neither person is well known to the priest, both may also be asked to submit two affidavits — obtained from either the parents, close relatives, or friends — attesting to the couple's freedom to enter into marriage.

In a mixed marriage, the Catholic partner is required to declare his or her intention to continue practicing the Catholic faith, and to do all in his or her power to share that faith with children born of the marriage by having them baptized and raised as Catholics.[3] In the past, the non-Catholic partner had to sign a document promising to raise the children of the union in the Catholic faith, but this is no longer the case. The non-Catholic partner must be informed, however, of the Catholic's declaration and promise.

Special Preparation — Remarriage

A situation of special concern to Catholics is when one (or both) of the prospective spouses has been previously married. As we mentioned earlier, the indissolubility of a valid marriage is one of the tenets of Catholicism. Although civil authorities and non-Catholic ministers consider divorced persons legally free to marry again, the Church still considers them married until a recognized Church authority declares otherwise. This is true whether the marriage involved two Catholics, a Catholic and a non-Catholic, or two non-Catholics. (Two non-Catholics remarrying falls outside Catholic Church jurisdiction, and therefore outside the concern of Catholic etiquette, as well.)

How can a second marriage take place in a Catholic church? Apart from widows and widowers, the answer lies in the annulment process. Any divorced person who wishes to marry a Catholic, or any divorced Catholic who wishes to remarry, must first determine whether the earlier marriage was actually valid, or whether some factor may have rendered it invalid from the start. Hidden impediments to the marriage, or an essential defect in consent or form, are some of the common reasons that Church authorities cite as grounds for a decree of nullity. In recent years, behavioral and psychological factors have been given greater attention, also.

Every diocese has procedures for initiating the annulment process, but the first step is to speak with your local pastor. Questionnaires and documents need to be filled out in some detail about the former marriage. While input and cooperation from the ex-spouse is helpful, it is not mandatory. These papers are usually then forwarded to a diocesan marriage tribunal, where they are carefully evaluated. Your local pastor may be able to offer advice specific to your situation about how far to proceed in making wedding plans during this waiting period, since processing times vary.

Annulments confuse most non-Catholics, causing some people to refer to them incorrectly as "Catholic divorces." For anyone involved in completing the paperwork, the process may also seem unnecessarily painful and cumbersome. This process, however, is the only way that Catholics are permitted to remarry and still participate in the sacraments of the Church.

Those Catholics who marry a divorced person, or who are themselves divorced and remarried without obtaining an annulment, often cause considerable discomfort to their Catholic friends and relatives. No matter how much we may care about the bride and groom personally, many devout Catholics find it difficult to participate in a wedding ceremony that the Church does not condone. Even if the divorced persons do not fully appreciate the need for an annulment, taking the time and effort to initiate the process will help alleviate serious concerns of the Catholics closest to them.

Announcements and Invitations

Once the date and place for a wedding have been set, and initial concerns resolved, the couple is often eager to share their news with friends and family. For the most part, Catholic couples can rely on standard etiquette guidelines to assist them with formulating the wording of the engagement announcement and wedding invitations. There are just a few unique issues that Catholics may encounter.

Marriage banns, a public announcement of the upcoming marriage at Mass on three consecutive Sundays, is an old custom that allowed anyone who knew of any reason why the engaged couple should not wed to come forth with that information. (This is the Catholic version of ". . . Speak now or forever hold your peace.") Many places still follow this custom, usually by posting the notice in the parish bulletin prior to the wedding, or making an announcement during Mass. Once the date has been set on the parish calendar, the church secretary will probably see that the banns get posted at the proper time. The banns are not usually proclaimed for an interfaith marriage, nor for the marriage of an older couple.

Catholics who are planning to marry in a valid non-Catholic ceremony may want to reassure their Catholic relatives and friends that the Catholic Church has approved their wedding plans. How can they convey this message with subtlety? One creative bride added the names of the ceremony co-officiants (one Presbyterian and one Catholic) on the invitation. This immediately, but tactfully, let her guests know that even though the wedding was scheduled to take place in a Presbyterian church, a Catholic priest would also be blessing the marriage. Other brides in these circumstances may want to follow her example.

In choosing attendants for the wedding ceremony, Catholics may select non-Catholics as well as Catholics to stand up for them. Unlike godparents or confirmation sponsors, Church law does not impose restrictions upon who may fulfill this duty. Similarly, Catholics may serve as honor attendants at a wedding for two non-Catholics without concern.

One type of wedding invitation or attendant request definitely poses special difficulties for devout Catholics, however — when a close Catholic friend or family member is planning to marry outside the Catholic Church, without procuring the necessary dispensation or annulment. In fact, this may be one of the most difficult etiquette questions Catholics (particularly those educated in the pre-Vatican II Church) may face. Each Catholic in this situation ultimately will have to make a personal decision about how best to respond, but I'd like to share a few points you may wish to consider.

The best initial approach may be to talk with your Catholic friend or relative early in the planning stage (or even pre-planning stage if possible), and encourage the couple to find out what steps may be required to obtain Church approval for their future wedding. Suggest they contact a local priest, or if you are especially close to the couple (a concerned parent, for example), you may even be able to gather some preliminary information to pass along to them. Perhaps you can show them that the process may not be quite as difficult or complex as they may have imagined.

If the couple disregards your tactfully presented suggestions and proceeds with their non-Catholic wedding plans, you then have several choices. You could express open disapproval and adamantly refuse to attend the wedding. Of course, this action will likely cause a permanent breach in your relationship with the bridal couple. A second option would be to ignore any problem and treat the invitation as you would any other. This behavior would preserve the friendship or family relationship, but may strike some Catholics as hypocritical or disrespectful of Church teaching. A middle-ground option may be to accept the invitation graciously and to pray fervently that God will continue to work in their lives. (No doubt most of us know of people who were only nominally Catholic, but became active participants in a Protestant church after a second marriage.) Be open to any opportunities that may arise later, when you may be able to advise them at a more receptive time about trying to obtain the Church's blessing on their marriage. If the issue still weighs heavily on you, talk with your pastor to see what advice he may offer. This is undeniably a sensitive issue, and one for which I can give no simple answers.

Planning the Ceremony

Weddings taking place in a Catholic Church may either be celebrated as part of a Nuptial Mass, or as a separate rite outside the context of a Mass. One of the first decisions the engaged couple must make, with the help of the priest, is whether or not their wedding ceremony will be a Mass. Generally, a Nuptial Mass is reserved for marriages where both bride and groom are Catholic, and the Rite of Marriage outside of Mass is used when one of the parties is non-Catholic. In some places the bishop may allow a mixed marriage to be celebrated as part of a Nuptial Mass, but it is rather unusual.

Once the Mass-vs.-no-Mass decision is made, the rest of the ceremony planning will flow from one of these two formats. Most priests give engaged couples a booklet or pamphlet to assist them in personalizing the rite, while remaining within the specified guidelines. Such booklets typically encourage the bride and groom to select Scripture readings, prayers, and the wording of the vows from among several acceptable choices.

Unlike many Protestant denominations, Catholic churches customarily impose strict limits on the type of musical selections that accompany the wedding ceremony. Sacred music alone — either classical or contemporary — is considered appropriate to the occasion. If the bride has her heart set on hearing one of her favorite popular love songs, or even "Here Comes the Bride," she'd better make arrangements to have them performed at the reception.

In addition to the attendants, Catholic weddings typically also include several other liturgical participants. The bride and groom customarily invite one or two honored guests to read the Scripture lessons during the ceremony. Readers may be family members, godparents, or close friends who have a clear and pleasant speaking voice. They need not be Catholic. Younger family members or friends may be asked to be altar servers, to assist the priest during various parts of the ceremony. These two or three boys or girls should be Catholic and already trained to carry out the altar-server duties. If no guests are able or willing to assume these roles, then the parish should be able to suggest possible candidates. When the Nuptial Mass is celebrated, a few additional participants are needed. Gift presenters carry the wine and bread to the priest prior to the Liturgy of the Eucharist. These honored guests may be family members or friends, adolescents or adults, but they should be Catholics who have already made their first Communion. Eucharistic ministers may also be needed to help the priest distribute Communion. Usually qualified guests are asked to serve as Eucharistic ministers for the Nuptial Mass, unless not enough guests have undergone the necessary training. In that case, the priest may suggest the names of parishioners who could assist, also.

The bride and/or groom should contact these selected friends and family members several weeks in advance to ask for their liturgical participation. Anyone who is invited to join the ceremony in one of these roles should consider it a rare privilege, and accept the honor graciously. If for some reason (major stage fright, for example) a guest feels unable or unwilling to perform the task, however, he or she may respectfully decline. In that case, the bride or groom must simply choose an alternative.

When a mixed marriage takes place in a Catholic church, it is sometimes possible for a non-Catholic minister to co-officiate part of the ceremony. Ask your parish priest if this might be workable for your situation. The priest would officiate for the exchange of vows, but the non-Catholic pastor could address, pray, and bless the couple. According to the "Bishops' Statement on Mixed Marriages," however, "It is not permitted to have two religious services or to have a single service in which both the Catholic marriage ritual and a non-Catholic marriage ritual are celebrated jointly or consecutively." [4] For weddings that take place in a non-Catholic church, the marriage rite outside of Mass may still be used, if it meets with the approval of the host clergy member. Since different denominations and pastors have different policies and preferences, check with the officiating pastors to find out what ceremony options may apply to your specific circumstances.

Other Wedding Preliminaries

Most of the non-ceremonial issues involved in planning a wedding, such as the guest list, choice of attire, and seating arrangements, do not have special Catholic etiquette concerns. A few areas are worth mentioning, however, as they may require some additional sensitivity in a Catholic wedding. In some parishes, these topics may be covered by specific policies and spelled out clearly to wedding planners. In other cases, the bride may want to ask the parish staff about local preferences prior to the wedding day, so that she can make arrangements accordingly. If a wedding consultant will be used, that person also should contact the parish staff in order to be advised of any particular preferences and/or restrictions.

Flowers — To avoid any disappointment or conflicts when decorating the church for the wedding, it's best to find out well in advance if there are any particular restrictions on floral decorations. During Lent, for example, many Catholic churches do not permit any flowers in the sanctuary. Other liturgical seasons have certain colors and decorations associated with them (for example, Christmas poinsettias or Easter lilies) and wedding floral arrangements should be planned around them.

Also, some churches allow flowers or other decorations to be fastened to pews; others have strict limits. Before making plans with your florist, check with your pastor or church secretary. At the same time, you may wish to ask whether any other weddings are scheduled for the same weekend. Some churches recommend that bridal parties consult with each other on appropriate altar and/or sanctuary flowers, and then share the cost between them.

Photography — Expect to encounter at least some restrictions on photography and videography during the liturgy, although specific policies vary from parish to parish. The pastoral concern is that flashes and scurrying photographers detract from the reverential mood of the wedding ceremony. In some churches, a professional photographer may be given more freedom than random guests. Whatever the policy, considerate couples will respect it and convey the restrictions clearly to their designated photographer, and to any guests with cameras.

Stipends — Wedding stipends are properly given not only to the presiding clergy, but to others who assist in the liturgy, also. Sometimes, parishes and participants have fixed fees established, but often it is up to the discretion of the ceremony sponsors. Ideally, stipends are commensurate with the size and scale of the wedding, and the amount of time the various individuals have contributed to the event. Customs vary widely from place to place, and family to family, but I've compiled a few general guidelines to assist the novice. Contact the parish secretary, however, to verify local practices.

Cantor and Organist — The ceremony hosts typically distribute these donations (fifty dollars and up) following the ceremony. Checks or cash should be prepared in advance, and placed in sealed envelopes. If the musicians are family friends, a thank-you note presented along with the donation would be a thoughtful gesture. Otherwise, a verbal thank-you with the donation should suffice.

Altar Servers — These gifts (five to twenty-five dollars) are usually presented by the best man on behalf of the bride and groom just prior to the ceremony. The groom should have the donations prepared in sealed envelopes, and give them to the best man at the rehearsal dinner or some other convenient time in advance of the wedding.

Priest — The groom typically gives the donation (one hundred dollars and up, placed in a sealed envelope) to the best man, who presents it to the priest following the ceremony. If in the form of a check, it should be made payable to the officiant personally. Please remember, this stipend is separate from any fee or donation paid for use of the church. If a co-officiant participates in the ceremony, a donation should likewise be presented to him or her, as well.

No stipends are necessary for those who serve as gift bearers, lectors, or Eucharistic ministers if they are selected from among the wedding guests. If they have been recruited from outside the guest list, however, a nominal gift would be appropriate.

The Ceremony

If the wedding is a Nuptial Mass, then most of the ceremony will follow the standard Mass liturgy outlined in Chapter Two, with the actual Rite of Marriage beginning after the homily. When the wedding takes place outside the Mass context, much of the Mass liturgy is omitted, although some elements (opening prayer, Scripture readings, and general intercessions, for example) remain in common. The pastor will review the specific ceremonial requirements and choices with the bride and groom, and with other members of the wedding party during the rehearsal.

What are the main components of the Catholic wedding rite? The actual marriage rite is quite brief, and consists of just three basic parts: the statement of intentions, consent and exchange of vows, and the blessing and exchange of rings.[5]

The minister asks the couple to state their intentions by answering three questions. 1) Will you love and honor each other as man and wife for the rest of your lives? 2) Have you come here freely and without reservation to give yourselves to each other in marriage? 3) Will you accept children lovingly from God, and bring them up according to the law of Christ and His Church? (Omitted for older couples.)

The pastor then states, "Since it is your intention to enter into marriage, join your right hands, and declare your consent before God and His Church." The couple exchanges vows, either using one of the prescribed formulas, or occasionally, vows they have written themselves. After the exchange, the minister says, "...What God has joined, men must not divide."

Finally, the minister blesses the wedding rings. The bride and groom then take turns placing the ring on their spouse's finger, while saying, "Take this ring as a sign of my love and fidelity."

One ritual that is not an official part of the Rite of Marriage but is sometimes included in a Catholic wedding is a gesture to honor Mary, the Mother of God. Often, the couple will walk over to a statue or picture of the Blessed Mother and deposit a bouquet of flowers. Other times the congregation may pray a Hail Mary or say the Memorare together. These rituals or a variation on them may be added to the service if the bride and groom wish. Usually, in a mixed marriage, this reference to Mary is left out, in deference to the many non-Catholics in attendance.

Receiving Line

One question ceremony sponsors may struggle with is whether or not to stage a receiving line in the vestibule of the church after the ceremony. Preferences vary, but the trend seems to be to opt out of a receiving line at the church. Alternatives are to have the bride and groom greet guests as they arrive at the church before the ceremony (non-traditional, but friendly), or more commonly, to form a receiving line at the reception instead. While it is important for the bride and groom to speak personally with each wedding guest, this can be accomplished by more than one method.

Reception

No matter how lavish or simple the post-wedding reception may be, it is appropriate to include the wedding officiant(s) as invited guests. This invitation should not be extended at the rehearsal or ceremony as an afterthought, but should be in the form of a written invitation mailed at the same time as those to your other guests. This gives the minister an opportunity to make plans to attend the reception, if he chooses. Though many will decline, it is a courtesy to issue the invitation anyway.

Navigating through all the various phases of Catholic wedding etiquette is not an easy task, especially when one of the parties is a new Catholic or a non-Catholic. Thankfully, parishes usually recognize this fact and make sure that the priest(s) and support staff do all they can to assist couples in preparing for, planning, and participating in the Sacrament of Matrimony. When it's all said and done, a Catholic wedding can be one of the most beautiful and meaningful celebrations that life has to offer. The few etiquette missteps that most of us inevitably make at some point along the way are rarely significant enough to mar the overriding joy of the day.

Endnotes

1. Catholic marriage law as quoted in *Our Sunday Visitor's 1996 Catholic Almanac*, Felician Foy, O.F.M. and Rose Avato, editors. Our Sunday Visitor Publishing Division, Huntington, Ind.: 1995, p. 234.
2. Ibid., p. 233.
3. "Implementation of the Apostolic Letter on Mixed Marriages," a statement approved by the National Conference of Catholic Bishops, 1970. Quoted in *The Catholic Almanac*, p. 235.
4. *The Catholic Almanac*, p. 235.

5. Some of this ceremony information was adapted from *The Two Shall be One: Preparing your Church Wedding* by Kathleen McAnany and Peter Schavitz, C.S.S.R. Ligouri Publications, Ligouri, Mo.: 1994.

ome Catholic traditions, customs, and etiquette associated with death have been drawn from the society around us, and are thus shared by the majority of Americans. Other common practices and condolence courtesies, however, are uniquely Catholic. These stem largely from Catholic beliefs about life, death, and the afterlife, and how these phases are intertwined. Also, as with other occasions, Catholic funeral rites incorporate numerous rituals and symbols to help express our beliefs in non-verbal ways.

Many cradle Catholics may not realize that some of these fundamental ideas and customs are not universally shared by their non-Catholic friends and neighbors. Likewise, many non-Catholics may feel at a loss as to how best to console a Catholic friend or family member when a death occurs. Certain standard phrases and gestures may seem odd, or even inappropriate, when used outside their respective religious cultures. Though some friends will brush off such blunders with an "it's the thought that counts" attitude, it may be disconcerting to others to find that a condolence sincerely offered somehow misses the mark, rather than offering genuine comfort during a difficult time.

Even when religious differences are not an issue, we may be uncertain about certain aspects of funeral protocol, because most of us (at least until a certain age) attend funerals only infrequently. The times we must be responsible for arranging a funeral are even rarer, and naturally fraught with emotion. When a death occurs in our immediate family or the immediate family of a close friend or associate, it is unlikely that we will have the time or inclination to go to the library or bookstore and find a book about funeral planning to peruse. Therefore, I encourage readers to resist the temptation to skip this chapter, even though the subject matter may be less appealing than previous topics. Then, when arrangements and courtesies associated with death become necessary tasks, you may be better prepared to deal with them.

In this chapter, we will look at issues and customs involved in planning a funeral ceremony for a loved one, and consider some of the responsibilities typically expected of the immediate family. We will also examine different protocol and etiquette guidelines for those outside the immediate family circle — friends and family who wish to console the chief mourners. In addition, we will see how different types of situations and circumstances may affect appropriate behavior.

Background

A key distinction between Catholic and Protestant theology concerns the efficacy of praying for the dead. During Protestant funeral services, ministrations and prayers are focused exclusively on the mourners. The prevailing doctrine is that the dead have already been judged, and are now beyond need of prayers offered by the living on their behalf. The loved ones left behind are the ones to whom we must direct our charity and concern.

In the Catholic funeral tradition, however, we not only comfort the bereaved, but we also pray for the deceased. The Catholic Church teaches that, "Though separated from the living, the dead are still at one with the community of believers on earth and benefit from (our) prayers and intercession." [1]

Integral to understanding this link between the living and

the dead is the Catholic concept of purgatory. In purgatory — a final purification of the elect after death — we must atone for sins committed during our lifetime. Catholics believe that by offering Masses, prayers, and good works, the living faithful can help hasten the departed's journey from purgatory to heaven.[2]

As we look now at traditions associated with death in a Catholic family, you can see how these beliefs are translated into specific practices.

Initial Contacts

When a loved one dies, it is obviously a time of great stress and emotion. It may be difficult to make decisions or know what to do, especially if the death is sudden. This is one reason why a priest should be summoned immediately. He can offer not only spiritual support, but also practical guidance about what steps need to be taken first. (If a priest is temporarily unavailable, he may ask a deacon or a lay bereavement minister to go in his place.)

Whether we are personally facing the death of a spouse, parent, or child, or whether we are stepping in to assist a close friend or neighbor in that situation, one of the first phone calls we make should be to the parish priest. If there is any doubt about which priest to call (or whether a non-Catholic minister would be preferred), a brief consultation with the other principals involved may be in order.

Generally, a Catholic survivor will want the support of a priest, even if the funeral itself will likely be a non-Catholic ceremony. Conversely, if the deceased is Catholic and the chief survivors are not, a priest should still be summoned to say prayers over the body. After the death of a loved one, Catholic family members often join with the priest to pray the Psalms and Scripture passages from the Office for the Dead section in the Liturgy of Hours, as an intercession for the one who has just died.[3] Given the different theological attitude toward prayers for the dead, we cannot ask a Protestant minister to perform this duty.

Another important task is notifying any immediate family members who are not already present. In most cases, they should simply be telephoned as soon as possible. While it is still preferable to deliver a death notification in person, this proves to be impractical in most families today, with members scattered across the country or even around the world. If we're especially concerned about how an elderly relative or other close survivor will take the news, perhaps we can contact a nearby friend or relative, a priest, or even a police officer who could convey the news in person. Be certain that this is done quickly, though, so that the relative we're trying to protect does not receive a disturbing phone call from someone else in the meantime.

Who makes these difficult notification calls? This depends on circumstances and the condition of the primary mourner(s). If we are close to the family, we can sometimes be a great help by offering to notify relatives and friends of the death. The important thing is to be sensitive to the feelings of the chief mourners (spouse, parent, or child) and use careful judgment. Sometimes the mourners may be too distraught to speak to anyone via phone; other times it is important to them to notify personally their family members and friends. Don't usurp the major survivor's right to make the calls, but offer to assume the task if asked.

Similarly, if we are in the position of the major survivor, and a well-meaning friend begins to make phone calls (or decisions) that we prefer to make ourselves, we should not hesitate to make our desires known. (This may be especially important if a non-Catholic friend takes charge.) Friends are there to support us, and sometimes they are searching for cues as to how they can best help. If we just sit back and say nothing, someone else will probably step in and do things their way.

Another person we'll probably want to contact is the funeral director. The priest or church office can suggest a reputable funeral home, if the family does not already have a strong preference. Most funeral homes, especially one recommended by the parish, have a basic understanding of common Catholic practices. Usually, the funeral home staff will pick up the body from the place of death and take it to their facility.

If the death has occurred far from where we wish to hold the funeral, a local funeral director can be invaluable in assessing the options and arranging to transport the body or remains. Experts caution against dealing with a distant funeral home via phone, particularly one picked at random from the yellow pages. A good local funeral director will have the contacts and knowledge of pertinent laws necessary to expedite the process, and may be able to save you much unwarranted expense.[4]

Organ donation, by the way, is consistent with Church teaching on charity, as long as the body is handled respectfully. In many places, medical personnel may routinely ask the survivors for permission to "harvest" usable organs.[5] By anticipating this request in advance, we may have a better idea of how we might wish to respond when the time comes. Some people find comfort in the fact that parts of their loved one's body can help sustain another's life, but others find it too discomfiting. This decision must be made quickly once death occurs, because timely removal of the organs is essential if they are to be of use to others.

Condolence Courtesies

Condolence flowers are a popular tradition among most Christian groups, although Catholic protocol is a bit unique. When sending flowers to Catholic mourners, we may either send them to the home of the bereaved or to the funeral home, if one is being used (marked "To the funeral of . . ."). It is not appropriate, however, to send flowers to a Catholic church with a similar notation. Why not? In Catholic churches, only a very few flowers, usually from the immediate family, are permitted. This is in keeping with the Catholic preference that religious symbolism not be overshadowed by "secular" symbols. (From a purely practical standpoint, I'm told the custodial staff typically does not like to mess with an excess of leftover flowers either, so many Protestant churches are adopting similar policies.)

While a room full of flowers is a beautiful tribute to the deceased and his or her family, some experts suggest sending a bouquet to the mourners several weeks after the funeral, when the family may be feeling particularly lonely. Others think flowers can express condolences in a way that words cannot express, and should therefore be sent immediately upon learning of the death. Some friends prefer to send live plants instead of flowers, so that the greenery can serve as a living reminder of the loved one. Any of these can be considerate gestures, unless the family specifies "no flowers" in the funeral announcement. In that case, we need to respect the family's expressed wishes.

A common Catholic condolence courtesy is arranging for a Mass to be said for the soul of the deceased. Catholics can easily arrange this through their own parish, or through any Catholic priest. In addition, certain religious orders routinely offer Masses for the deceased, usually providing a card with which to notify the family and a Mass request form to fill out and return.[6] Some families keep a supply of these on hand, to send in when an occasion arises. Although not mandatory, a nominal donation (five to twenty dollars) is customarily included with any Mass intention request.

A person of any religion may arrange for a Mass to be said, but it may feel awkward for someone who does not share the Catholic faith. Non-Catholics may prefer to send a memorial donation to a charity or organization that they feel more comfortable supporting. This donation should be in keeping with the wishes of the deceased and/or the family, however, not just one's own church or favorite organization. A donation to the

ASPCA, for example, when the deceased never showed much affection for animals, would not be nearly as welcome as a comparable donation to the charity designated by the survivors, or one to which the deceased devoted much time and effort.

Taking food to the home of the bereaved is another time-honored custom in many communities. Upon learning of the death, neighbors and friends prepare dishes that can be served to the relatives and close friends who will soon gather at the home of the deceased and/or the immediate survivor(s). Sometimes this is an organized gesture, as when a group of neighbors or co-workers plan a meal together. Other times, friends drop over individually with items that can easily be served and shared. Catholic dietary restrictions should not be a factor, unless we're bringing food on Friday. Meat is strictly prohibited only on Fridays during Lent (and Ash Wednesday), but some Catholics maintain the tradition of meatless Fridays throughout the year.

A few basic gestures can be offered and appreciated by mourners of any faith. Simply anticipating or recognizing the needs of the family and unobtrusively helping to meet them may alleviate some of the typical stress and chaos surrounding a death. For example, offering to help care for the youngest children, either at our home or the home of the bereaved, may free the parents and grandparents to focus on other tasks. Offering to meet out-of-town visitors at the airport and/or helping to arrange for their meals and accommodations is another thoughtful gesture, especially in large and widely-scattered families.

Under certain circumstances, helping to clean or tidy up the home of the deceased and/or the chief survivor(s) prior to the arrival of guests may be genuinely appreciated. Sometimes the weeks preceding death have been devoted to caring for a critically ill patient and routine housework has been understandably neglected. For some, the thought of numerous friends and relatives seeing the home in such a state causes additional stress. Others may see it as a trivial concern.

Approach the subject tactfully with the family. Offer to come in and clean (alone or with another trusted friend, family member, or employee) while the family is at the funeral home, perhaps. Bringing our own cleaning supplies or learning where they're kept will minimize any further intrusion, also. If the survivor seems grateful for the suggestion, we can proceed. If, however, he or she seems reluctant or uncomfortable with the idea, we should not pursue the matter any further. We must respect the family's privacy, and their right to accept or reject any offers of assistance.

Preliminary Planning

Numerous people nowadays, especially the elderly, have taken steps to pre-plan their funeral arrangements. Anyone assisting in making funeral arrangements should, therefore, ascertain first whether the deceased may have left instructions regarding death. Presumably, any instructions of this kind, and their location, will have been made explicit to the likely survivor(s) ahead of time. Catholics who will be leaving primarily non-Catholic survivors may want to make sure their wishes regarding Catholic funeral practices are made known. (Incidentally, funeral information should not be recorded in the will, because that document ordinarily will not be read until after the burial.)

If no pre-arrangements have been made, the priest or his representative should be able to guide us through the necessary planning steps, outlining some of the options, and explaining the preliminary decisions which need to be made. A "standard" Catholic funeral, as specified in the *Order of Christian Funerals* (promulgated in 1989), actually consists of three separate ceremonies: the Vigil Service, the Funeral Liturgy, and Committal. In addition, the *Order* suggests a rite for prayers immediately after death, a brief prayer service at the first gathering in the presence of the body (after it has been prepared for viewing), and again when the family and close friends prepare to accompany the body to the church or place of committal. There are several variations and possible combinations of these rites, however, so each funeral will be somewhat unique, depending on the needs and preferences of the family.

The Funeral Mass (or Funeral Liturgy, if a Mass is not desired) is the main liturgical service, and should be the starting point around which other plans are made. Some days (primarily Sundays during Advent, Lent, and the Easter season, Holy Days of Obligation, and Thursday, Friday, and Saturday during Holy Week) are prohibited for Catholic Funeral Masses, so dates may need to be adjusted accordingly. Usually, the Vigil Service takes place at the funeral home the evening before the funeral, although it can be arranged at the home of the deceased or at the church, also. The Rite of Committal customarily takes place at the cemetery, either at the gravesite or in an internment chapel on the premises.

The Wake

Though not mandated by Catholic custom or theology, contemporary American bereavement practices often involve calling hours at a funeral home for one or two days prior to the funeral.[7] This allows friends and extended family members to offer condolences to the immediate family. The casket is usually present, but may be either open or closed. Commonly called a wake, this time may be referred to as "visitation" or "viewing."

Historically, wakes were held at the dead person's home,[8] and that is still an acceptable, though less common, alternative to the funeral home. Some families prefer to receive visitors at their home, but leave the body elsewhere. Other families arrange for calling hours at the church, either with or without the casket in view. Specific arrangements often depend on the circumstances of death, the estimated number of visitors, and family preferences. Reliance on the funeral home setting also seems to differ somewhat by region and ethnic group as well.

If the wake does take place at a funeral home, much of the procedure will be "generic," and non-reflective of the deceased's religious affiliation. A few practices are specific to Catholics, however, and may be confusing to non-Catholic visitors. Similarly, Catholic callers at a non-Catholic wake may be surprised at the absence of certain familiar traditions.

One important distinction is the *prie-dieu* (a padded bench suitable for kneeling in prayer) located in front of the casket. When Catholic mourners and supporters visit the funeral parlor, it is customary to kneel on the *prie-dieu* for a few minutes praying for the deceased. Vigil lights and a crucifix are usually arranged near the casket to facilitate prayer. Non-Catholic visitors may kneel if they wish, but it is not necessary.

Another custom associated with Catholicism is the practice of having a commemorative holy card (also called a memorial card or prayer card) imprinted with an appropriate prayer or Scripture verse. The card includes the name of the deceased, his or her birth and death dates, and sometimes a photograph as well. Other times, a religious picture is featured in lieu of a photograph. These are usually displayed by the guest register book, and visitors may take a card home as a keepsake and as a reminder to pray for the departed.

In the past, I did not realize the significance attached to these memorial cards, and treated them somewhat carelessly. Perhaps I mentally lumped them into the same category as imprinted napkins from weddings, or inscribed matchbook covers from anniversary parties — inexpensive souvenirs of the day. Now that I have a better understanding of this practice, however, I know why devout Catholics often keep these holy cards tucked into Bibles or favorite prayer books. It is a tangible reminder of the deceased that encourages us continually to remember the departed in our prayers. Parents of young children may want to take extra cards to save and pass along to the children when they are old enough to participate in this discipline, also.

Visitors to a wake frequently wonder, "What should I say?" Often a simple "I'm sorry" is eloquent enough; our presence speaks for itself. Traditionally, visitors were expected to wait to speak to a mourner until the mourner spoke first. Today, this may not be strictly observed, but it's best to approach the survivor(s) silently. After the mourner greets us, either by word or gesture, we may offer condolences.

A few comments should be specifically avoided when speaking to Catholic mourners. Following death, Protestants often speak with great certainty that "We know he/she is in heaven now." As alluded to earlier, Catholic theology is more complex, and the exact state of the soul less assured in Catholic thinking. Though tempting to comfort the bereaved with such words, a more appropriate phrase may be "He/she certainly seemed to lead a faith-filled life," or some similar expression. When sincerely delivered, these words could bring comfort and reassurance to the bereaved Catholic, without contradicting either party's religious beliefs.

Another comment that one sometimes hears at the funeral home is "He/she looks almost alive," or the equally banal, "Doesn't it seem as if he/she is just sleeping?" While these may attest to the skill of the undertakers, any comments which attempt to deny death or minimize the loss of life, should be considered inappropriate.

Vigil Service

The evening before a funeral, Catholics customarily hold a vigil for the deceased. Prior to 1989, when the new *Order of Christian Funerals* was issued, families simply gathered and recited the rosary together. Recognizing that many non-Catholics feel uncomfortable with the rosary, however, the *Order of Christian Funerals* suggests a Scripture-based vigil service. This service may be held at the funeral home toward the end of the visitation hours, or at the church, either following calling hours or independent of them. It is usually led by a priest or deacon, although when no priest or deacon is available, a layperson may preside.[9] At times, the family may wish to have the vigil at the home of the deceased or bereaved instead. In this case, the format can be shortened and simplified, if desired.

Usually, the vigil service is open to anyone who wishes to attend, and the newspaper's death notice will include the time and place. Some people who will be unable to come to the funeral the next day may wish to attend the evening service. This gives them an opportunity to pray with the family in an organized way, in addition to offering personal condolences. Many, however, will attend both the vigil and the funeral service, especially family members and close friends.

The full vigil service includes Scripture readings, hymns, a short homily, prayers, and if desired, the recitation of the rosary (although the *Order* itself does not mention it). The *Order of Christian Funerals* also suggests a time of family remembrance in the rubrics, where those gathered share with each other memories of the deceased. Depending on the size and formality of the gathering, this can either be done in an organized format with specific individuals asked in advance to prepare a few words, or more spontaneously, with everyone invited to reminisce in their own way. This sharing of memories may also be arranged outside of the vigil service context, in a more informal way. Sometimes, a display of mementoes or photos of the deceased helps trigger the reminiscing.

Other personalized touches and informalities which would not be considered appropriate at a Funeral Mass can sometimes be included in the less formal vigil service. For example, songs or music that held special significance for the deceased, but are outside the traditional sacred music repertoire, might be effective during the vigil, especially when scheduled outside of the parish church setting.

When the vigil is held in the church, the introductory rites include the reception of the casket and the corresponding rituals. When the vigil is held elsewhere these rites are omitted, forming the beginning of the funeral service the next day instead. (These are described in more detail below.)

The Funeral — Planning

A priest can conduct the funeral liturgy either in the context of a Mass or outside of Mass, depending on family preference and the relationship of the deceased to the Church. A Funeral Mass, the preferred choice of most Catholic families, is customarily held in the parish church of the deceased or his/her family. In some dioceses, a Mass can occasionally be held at the funeral home, but in other dioceses Mass is limited to a church setting.

If many of the mourners are non-Catholic, the family may choose to have a funeral liturgy without a Mass to help them feel more comfortable with the service, and to avoid any potential misunderstandings about Catholic Communion restrictions.[10] The liturgy outside of a Mass context may be conducted either at the funeral home or at church.

Regardless of which option we choose, family members can expect to play an active role both in planning and participating in the funeral. Similar to what was described in the last chapter regarding wedding Masses, the principal ceremony planners are encouraged to select Scripture readings from among a number of appropriate choices, and identify which hymns and music they wish to use. They also typically invite specific relatives or friends to serve as lectors, gift bearers, and Eucharistic ministers.

If we are asked to assume one of these roles, we should consider it an honor and accept graciously. Some of us, however, may feel too overcome by grief to be able to read clearly or assist with the service on this occasion. In that case, we may suggest that someone who is a bit less emotionally involved be asked instead. The chief survivor should be able to respect our discomfort and find a suitable replacement. If no friends or family are willing to assume these roles, then trained members of the parish may be contacted.

At larger funerals, some mourners (usually six to ten) may be invited to serve as pallbearers. This may either be an honorary role (with the funeral home staff or other pallbearers actually lifting the casket), or a working role, where the duty of carrying the casket in and out of church falls to these selected friends and relatives. Traditionally, pallbearers have been men, but today women may also be asked to serve in this capacity (although it is still quite rare). Non-Catholics as well as Catholics may be pallbearers at a Catholic funeral. Similarly, Catholics may serve as pallbearers for a non-Catholic funeral whenever they are asked.

Unless the ceremony planner instructs otherwise, pallbearers wear dark suits (or dark dresses). This group customarily sits together during the funeral in the front of the church, so spouses and/or companions of pallbearers should expect to sit separately. Usually pallbearers are asked to arrive a bit early and meet with the priest and/or funeral home staff prior to the start of the service. If uncertain about genuflecting in the aisle or any other protocol, ask the priest or other knowledgeable person at this time.

Sometimes, other friends and relatives may be asked to serve as ushers for the funeral. These people help seat the attendees, generally ensuring that the seats up front are filled first. (The very front pews, however, are always reserved for the immediate family.) At some funerals, the funeral home personnel may act as ushers. At others, no ushers are deemed necessary and visitors simply seat themselves.

Parish musicians usually have an established fee for their services. This may be paid directly by the family or paid by the funeral home and then billed to the family. For the priest and/or deacon, the family should have a stipend envelope prepared in advance, and a representative of the family can present it before or after the funeral services. (Sometimes the funeral home staff will deliver it upon request, also.) Again, stipend amounts vary widely across the country, but the typical range is probably from fifty to one hundred fifty dollars. The amount of time devoted to helping the family during the death and funeral process, as well as family circumstances, should be taken into account when determining a reasonable honorarium.

Additional Considerations

An additional planning consideration that arises in many families is, "What do we do with the children?" No clear-cut answers can be offered to this question because circumstances, family attitudes, and individual children vary so much. Some families may think it inappropriate for young children, grand-children, or great-grandchildren to attend the funeral, while others will welcome the presence of the youngest generation. Similarly, some children will handle the death and its ceremonies with a maturity beyond their years, while other children may be traumatized by the sight of an open casket.

Decisions should be based on the age and maturity level of our children, how close they were to the deceased, and how we think the chief survivors may react to their presence. Sometimes it's difficult to determine whether the children will cope better by being included or excluded from the funeral rites. All we can do is use our best judgment, and then continue to monitor the effects of grief after the funeral, offering as much support and reassurance as possible. As with other church services, we should take the children out any time they become too disruptive.

Parents of infants and toddlers may face limited options for child care, especially if they have traveled some distance to attend the funeral. When my husband's grandmother died, I remember struggling to keep my one-year-old out of trouble at the funeral home, struggling to keep him quiet during a Funeral Mass that coincided with his customary meal time, and struggling to keep him warm at the cemetery. I would have preferred to leave him in someone else's care for a few hours, but the only people I knew in town were also attending the funeral. Staying home from the funeral to care for my child seemed an unacceptable alternative, since my absence would almost certainly have offended my in-laws.

In this type of situation, a neighbor or friend of the family could help immensely by offering to line up a reliable babysitter for out-of-town guests, or assuming child care responsibility personally, if attending the funeral does not take precedence. Making arrangements to use the church nursery or a semiprivate space at the funeral home to care for the younger children may also be a welcome gesture. Some families may prefer to keep the children with the parents, however, rather than leave them with someone unfamiliar during this time. We can approach the family with a clear offer of child-care assistance, then let them decide whether or not to accept our offer.

Another potentially troublesome issue that may need to be considered is whether or not cremation will be a factor in the funeral process. Until just recently, cremation posed particular concerns to Catholics, often complicating plans for a Catholic Funeral Mass and leaving priests and families at odds. Although the longstanding ban against cremation was lifted in 1963, ashes were still generally not permitted at Funeral Masses,[11] because Church law required that the urn or box containing the ashes be left outside the church (usually in a funeral car). As one veteran pastor explained, "Priests were put in the awkward position of telling the families of the deceased they had to leave the remains at the curb."[12] In a situation where emotions are already running high, such a disagreement about how to handle the funeral can only compound the family's anguish and distress.

Recognizing that this was a growing problem for pastors and families, the United States bishops voted in June 1996 to ask the Vatican for a nationwide exception to this prohibition. While emphasizing that the ideal way to have a body cremated is to have it incinerated after the Funeral Mass, they also realize that the expense of transporting a body from a distant place of death to a funeral site often forces many people to ship the cremated remains back home instead. Checking with a priest *before* making any decisions about the disposal of a loved one's body should help minimize misunderstandings or conflict at the time of the funeral.

Another sensitive issue involves recording the funeral. Though I was unaware of the practice until researching this book, some families or funeral homes apparently record the funeral either on audio or video for distribution to out-of-town guests who could not attend the services, or for family archival purposes. Perhaps in some cases, a recording of the event may be desirable (for example, where the surviving spouse in a traffic accident cannot leave the hospital and wants to view the funeral via tape), but many mourners are likely to be offended at the idea, regardless of who commissions it. Although news photographers seem to do it routinely, filming someone who is openly expressing grief still ranks as an invasion of privacy. I doubt that many Catholic priests would allow recording equipment at a funeral, except under compelling circumstances.

The Funeral

If the body has not already been received at the church as part of the vigil service, the rite of reception begins the Funeral Mass (or Funeral Liturgy). This is a simple yet beautiful rite, rich in symbolism. First the minister sprinkles the coffin with holy water "in remembrance of the deceased person's initiation and first acceptance into the community of faith."[13] Next, if it is the custom in the local community, the immediate family members, close friends, or the minister drape a white pall (a heavy cloth) over the casket. This, too, is reminiscent of the white baptismal garment, and can be a way for the survivors to offer a final "service" to the deceased.

The entrance procession follows, including the ceremony participants and the pallbearers. Sometimes family members wish to place a Christian symbol or symbols on the pall, such as a Bible, a book of the Gospels, or a cross. If so, selected representatives of the family carry these items in the procession, then lay them on the pall at the conclusion of the procession. Only Christian items are permitted in this ritual. Flags, organizational insignias, or secular items of any kind are not allowed on the casket, at least while it is in the church. (An exception is the funeral of a child.)

Then the funeral proceeds according to the Mass outline given in Chapter Two, with Scripture readings, hymns, a homily, prayers, and Communion, or omitting Communion in the case of the funeral outside of Mass. At a Catholic funeral, the officiant's homily speaks about what Scripture tells us in general about death and resurrection, rather than focusing on the specific attributes or accomplishments of the deceased. For some, this can convey a rather impersonal tone, although it reflects the explicit intentions of the *Order.*

In an effort to make the Funeral Mass more personally meaningful to those gathered, a representative of the family may be asked to say something about the life of the deceased. The family decides who, if anyone, in addition to the clergy may speak at the service. Unlike spontaneous reminiscences that may have been offered at the vigil service, this is a more formal speech, in keeping with the overall tone of the Mass or liturgy. While not labeled as a "eulogy" by the *Order*, this "spoken remembrance" serves much the same function. According to standard etiquette, this talk should not rival the homily in length, but range from three to seven minutes, with about five minutes considered ideal. [14]

After the remembrance, a final commendation prayer and hymn conclude the funeral. As a farewell gesture, and as a sign of respect or reverence, the priest incenses the casket. Holy water may be sprinkled also, although this is usually omitted if the casket was sprinkled during the rite of reception at the beginning of the Mass. The priest and assisting ministers then lead the procession out of the church, with the coffin, the family and other mourners following.

Committal

The third and last ceremony outlined in the *Order of Christian Funerals* is the rite of committal. It may be celebrated at the grave, tomb, or crematorium, or even at sea. There are several variations of this rite, depending on whether it immediately follows the funeral or is celebrated independently of the funeral. (Sometimes a funeral is held in one city, for example, and burial in another.) It is basically a brief service of prayer, with perhaps a song at the end.

Where it is the custom, some sign or gesture of leave-taking may be made. Usually, this is done systematically with mourners queuing around the casket, and placing flowers or soil on the coffin. This may be made clear ahead of time, or we may just follow the lead of those for whom the custom is more familiar. Often the presiding minister makes an announcement that the family would like to invite everyone in attendance to some kind of meal immediately following.

The Funeral Meal

Friends and family rarely just disperse from the cemetery or the church, but gather together following the services to share memories of the deceased and enjoy a meal together. This may be at a restaurant, at the parish hall, at the home of the deceased, or at some other convenient location. When one of their fellow members dies, parishioners frequently prepare and serve food for the funeral dinner. (If a parish group provides a dinner after the funeral, an optional donation can be sent to the parish for that ministry, along with a thank-you note.) Other times, friends or neighbors may make meal arrangements for the guests. Whatever the specific arrangements, the priest should be invited to join the mourners at this meal. Sometimes the atmosphere at the funeral dinner may become quite jolly, as family and friends celebrate life in the midst of death.

After the Funeral

In the weeks following the funeral, the survivors write thank-you notes to those who have participated in the funeral service, and those who offered various condolences. This task can be shared among the principal survivors and need not fall exclusively on one person. In the case of elderly survivors, another person (family or friend) can offer to assist in actually writing a note that the elderly person dictates. This is especially appreciated by those who may have a physical problem, such as arthritis, that makes writing painful. Family and friends should continue to remember the grieving both in prayer, and in deed. Sometimes a short note, telephone call, or bouquet several weeks after the funeral means as much or more to the survivors as those that are sent immediately.

Catholics have the additional obligation to remember the deceased, as well as the bereaved, in our thoughts and prayers. At each Mass, we pray not only for the living, but also for those who have departed this life. One of the consoling factors of the Catholic faith is the belief that the communion of saints transcends death and allows us to maintain a connection with those who have gone before us. Our relationship with our loved ones changes significantly when death separates us, but the connection does not die.

Endnotes

1. *Order of Christian Funerals*, prepared by the International Commission on English in the Liturgy. Catholic Book Publishing Company, New York: 1989, no. 6.
2. For more information on the concept of purgatory, refer to the *Catechism*, nos. 1030-1032. Also, "The Sweet Pain of Purgatory" by Mark Shea in the September/October 1996

issue of *Catholic Heritage* (pp. 10-12) reviews current Church teaching on this topic.

3. These prayers are also listed in the *Order of Christian Funerals.*

4. Young, Gregory, *The High Cost of Dying.* Prometheus Books, Buffalo, New York: 1994.

5. *Our Sunday Visitor's Catholic Almanac*, Felician A. Foy, O.F.M. and Rose Avato, editors. Our Sunday Visitor Publishing Division, Huntington, Ind.: 1995, p. 56.

6. Two organizations that offer Masses for the deceased are: Sacred Heart Monastery, P.O. Box 900, Hales Corners, WI 53130; and The Spiritans, Holy Ghost Fathers, Brothers and Associates, 11411 Amherst Ave., Wheaton, MD 20902.

7. American families, however, do not follow this custom if they are Jewish. Instead, burial takes place quickly, within twenty-four hours, then the family sits shivah for up to seven days at home following the burial. Friends and extended- family members make condolence calls at this time. It is appropriate to bring food, but not flowers, to Jewish mourners. For more information, see Helen Latner's *The Book of Modern Jewish Etiquette*, Schocken Books: 1981.

8. The Hebrews began the idea of the Vigil for the Dead, or wake, as a means of guarding against premature burial. Family and friends stood watch for any signs of life. The custom was continued by Christians in the middle ages as an act of piety. Information from *Catholic Book of the Dead* by Ann Ball. Our Sunday Visitor Publishing Division, Huntington, Ind.: 1995, p. 47.

9. *Order of Christian Funerals*, no. 14.

10. Parish custom regarding reminders about Catholic Communion restrictions vary. Some pastors make an announcement; others omit any direct reference. The official policy as established by the National Conference of Bishops is given in Chapter Two, p. 45.

11. In a few areas of the United States (Pueblo, Colorado; Reno,

Nevada; and Honolulu, Hawaii) local bishops had requested and been granted a Vatican "indult" or permission to overlook this stipulation.

12. Father James Setelik, quoted by Robert Holton in "To Comfort Mourners, New Cremation Rules." *Our Sunday Visitor*, July 21, 1996, p. 3.

13. *Order of Christian Funerals*, no. 133. As Michael Marchal notes in *Parish Funerals* (Liturgy Training Publications, Archdiocese of Chicago: 1987), "In the rites we inherited from the medieval church, holy water seemed to be used primarily for exorcism or absolution. Now it is a proclamation of the death and life into which the deceased entered through the waters of baptism."

14. Baldrige, Letitia, *Complete Guide to the New Manners for the '90's*. Rawson Associates, New York: 1990, p. 339.

Chapter Twelve
Daily and Seasonal Catholic Living

*I*n the preceding chapters we have looked at the major ceremonial celebrations of the Catholic Church, and some of the etiquette issues commonly associated with them. Not all of Catholic life, nor all of our etiquette concerns, are limited to weekend Masses or predictable rites of passage, however. In this chapter, we will examine some of the daily and seasonal ways in which Catholicism colors (and at times complicates) our lives.

Both within the parish and among our wider circle of friends, family, and associates, we can expect to face some awkward situations where we feel caught between loyalty to our faith and loyalty to our relationships. At times, the challenge may come from those who do not appreciate our beliefs or traditions. Other times, we may be flustered by those who do not seem to realize that we need some time away from the parish, also.

Simultaneously respecting the rules of the faith and the rules of polite society can seem impossible at times. When the two codes conflict, we may be forced to make some uncomfortable choices, and at times difficult confrontations. Such situations are "messy" and often there are no simple answers. I can say confidently, however, that these conflicts will be easier to handle when we first develop a clear understanding of our own beliefs and priorities. Then, we must explain — firmly but tactfully — to others involved why we feel compelled to respond in a certain way. While this method is not guaranteed to prevent hurt feelings or misunderstandings, most people can appreciate and respect an honest yet thoughtful approach.

The following questions address some of these areas where conflicts most frequently arise. Reading through these questions and answers may help you formulate ideas about how you would handle similar situations in your own life. With a combination of awareness and sensitivity, we should be able to gracefully bridge our religious and social lives without making (too many) unwanted compromises.

Catholic Education

Q: Our neighbors think we're crazy to bus our child to the Catholic school across town when "one of the best schools in the state" is within walking distance. Furthermore, they do not hesitate to voice this opinion frequently, often within earshot of our children. I would like to maintain some of these friendships with my neighbors, especially for my children's sake, but I'm finding it hard to hold my tongue. What can I say to these people, or do I simply say nothing?

A: First, realize that some contemporary suburban neighborhoods are drawn together largely by the fact that the residents there selected the same area or subdivision based upon the reputation of the local schools. Since this is a key bonding point, they are upset by anyone who challenges the neighborhood "group-think" by enrolling their children elsewhere.

Recognizing that this is the context in which your neighbors are questioning your decision should help formulate your response.

Find a time when you can speak privately with one or two neighborhood friends whose friendship you most value. Let them know that their derogatory comments about your family's school choice trouble you. Mention, too, that you're concerned about how such remarks may undermine your children's confidence or attitude toward their school. In your conversation, remain positive about the neighborhood and your friendship, reassuring them that the local school is undeniably an important asset to the area. Voice optimism that your family and theirs can still share many common interests independent of the school system.

Be frank, though, in explaining that you chose a Catholic school because of the values, atmosphere, and religious instruction that simply cannot be offered in any public school. Also, make it clear that your decision has already been made, so you do not appreciate a realtor-type sales pitch on the merits and convenience of the neighborhood school. Likewise, you should make a pledge, either silently or to your friends, that you will not denigrate the public school in front of your children, either. School choice need not be a source of friction, unless parents feel compelled to justify their own decision by attacking the alternative(s).

Christmas Cards

Q: Each Christmas I struggle with the decision about what type of greeting card to buy. We have a wide circle of friends and associates, including Catholics, Protestants, Jews, and some with no religious affiliation. The increasingly popular "Seasons Greetings" cards have always seemed too secular, but I'm wondering now if those are the only "politically correct" cards to send today.

A: In so many ways, Christmas has already been transformed into a secular "American" holiday, and the increasing popularity of cards that blend "Happy Hanukah," "Merry Christmas," and "Happy New Year" into one generic greeting seems one more step in that direction. For that reason, I have always selected a Christmas card with a distinctly religious message to send to most of my friends and relatives.

On the other hand, I have also become increasingly aware that greeting cards are not only a message *from* us (and therefore naturally reflective of our own taste and beliefs), but also a message *to* someone else whose taste and beliefs must also be considered if we are truly being courteous. For example, for several years I received unusually beautiful Christmas cards each year from a friend in Japan who never celebrated Christmas herself. I treasured these cards not only for their beauty but also for their uniqueness, because I knew she sent New Year's cards to all of her other friends, yet specifically searched the Tokyo stores for a Christmas card to send to me.

With a heightened sensitivity toward the recipients of my Christmas greetings, therefore, I have recently begun purchasing several different cards for use each year. I usually buy some with a definite Catholic look,[1] some with a more Protestant slant (no halos on Mary or Joseph), and a few non-religious cards, also. As I go through my list, I select the card which I think is most appropriate for each name. From my viewpoint, this practice does not add to the secularization trend, but does demonstrate respect for a diversity of traditions.

By the way, I encourage everyone to add a personal note with the cards, whenever possible. A friend once told me that opening a Christmas card and finding only a signature is for her like opening a gift box and discovering it's empty. I agree. For me, even a short, quickly scrawled note across the back of the card boosts its value immensely.

Inviting a Pastor to Dnner

Q: I was raised in a Protestant tradition in which it was customary to invite the pastor and his wife for dinner occasionally. Now, I'm Catholic and would like to include the parish priest at our dinner table some evening, but feel awkward about inviting him. Is this proper among Catholics, or is this strictly a Protestant tradition? Do you think the priest would appreciate such an invitation, or would it just be uncomfortable for all of us?

A: Go ahead and invite him. Expect that his schedule is busy, however, so you may want to offer him a choice of several times and dates. Inviting a priest to dinner is a tradition that used to be more common in Catholic circles, but seems less popular today, perhaps because family mealtimes are often hurried or eaten in shifts nowadays as family members rush to different activities.

A shared meal may provide a good opportunity for you and him to get to know each other better, and for your children (if you have any) to see the priest welcomed in your home. Actually, I've wanted to issue such an invitation myself for several years, but keep waiting until my children's table manners improve! Therefore, I can empathize with your hesitancy, but I encourage you to follow your hospitable instincts.

Prayer at Dinner Parties

Q: My husband and I like to entertain, and frequently host dinner parties at our home for about six to eight guests. Is it appropriate to say grace before beginning the meal at these parties? My husband thinks because table prayer is a daily custom in our household, we should continue the custom regardless of who may or may not be joining us. I'm concerned that our usual, "Bless us O Lord, and these thy gifts. . ." makes some guests uncomfortable because the words (and sign of the cross) are unfamiliar to them. Isn't the primary job of a host and hostess to make their guests comfortable and at ease?

A: You're correct in recognizing that this is a situation where sensitivity as well as custom should come into play. At intimate dinner parties where guests share a common (or similar) religious heritage, your customary table blessing would be perfectly appropriate. When we gather at my parents' home, for example, everyone says (or listens to) the Protestant grace; when the family gathers at our home, my husband often leads us in saying (or listening to) the Catholic pre-meal prayer.

At dinner parties that go beyond our immediate family or parish group, however, we need to demonstrate some additional sensitivity for a diversity of traditions and beliefs. Secular etiquette experts generally discourage a group table prayer at dinner parties of six or more people, and I think this is probably sound advice. A personal silent prayer before eating should satisfy our own devotional need, without imposing upon our guests.

Lenten Abstinence

Q: One Friday evening during Lent, I happened to be seated conspicuously at the head table in a large Protestant gathering. When the waiter brought a plate of filet mignon and set it in front of me, I froze. No other entree choices were offered, but no one else seemed bothered by that fact. Was I right to violate the rule of Friday abstinence, or should I have risked offending my hosts by leaving the meat on my plate?

A: In my opinion, you were correct under the circumstances in graciously eating the meal that had been served. Hopefully, you then substituted the following day (or two) as your Lenten abstinence for the week. The situation as you describe it indicates no malice or "test" on the part of your hosts, but simply an unawareness of this common Catholic discipline. To leave the plate untouched could have deeply embarrassed your hosts, and unnecessarily offended those around you.

While Catholics are obliged to refrain from eating meat on

Ash Wednesday and all the Fridays during Lent, this is designed to be a private act of devotion and self-discipline, not a public display of our ecumenical differences. Now that you are more aware of this potential problem, however, you may be able to avoid future difficulty by inquiring in advance about menu plans when accepting any invitations for Fridays during Lent.

Protestant Proselytizing

Q: I'm feeling increasingly frustrated by my evangelical neighbors who seemed determined to "convert" my children. Although we are active in our local Catholic parish, the neighbors' church plans all kinds of fun activities for children and families that are not available through our church. At first, I was pleased when these friends offered to take my preschoolers to Vacation Bible School or invited us to the annual ice cream social. Now, however, as the children are getting older, they are coming home with pamphlets and ideas that sometimes run counter to our Catholic theology. I've become more and more uneasy with the invitations, but don't know quite how to refuse them. What do you suggest?

A: Some religious groups practice genuine hospitality, while others use hospitality as a means of recruiting new members. Without determining precisely which of these categories your neighbors fall into, you must respect your own instincts. If you're concerned that peer pressure is being subtly or directly applied to your children, then it is time to put a limit on their involvement with the evangelical church.

Politely refusing invitations is never easy. Politely refusing repeated invitations is even harder. For this reason, I recommend a direct approach. Tell your neighbors that you appreciate their friendship and willingness to include your family in their church-sponsored activities, but that you feel your children are at an age now where they are likely to be confused by differing theologies. Suggest that you get together in a secular setting, if you and they want to maintain the relationship.

Visiting Shrines

Q: My family was traveling around the midwest on a vacation last summer when we realized from a map that we were near a popular Marian shrine. On the spur of the moment, we decided to visit. We were startled to learn upon arrival that there was a strict dress code, however, and we were not permitted to enter. Is this typical of shrines? For future reference, how do I find out about these restrictions so we can plan accordingly?

A: Visiting shrines or other places of devotional interest can be an interesting and worthwhile side trip or addition to a vacation. The dress restrictions you encountered are not unusual for this type of site, though, so some advance planning is necessary. For example, some places require head coverings for women; others refuse to allow bare shoulders anywhere within the immediate vicinity of the shrine.

The *Our Sunday Visitor's Catholic Almanac*[3] annually compiles a list of shrines and other places of special significance to Catholics. Shrines are grouped by state, and entries include addresses. If time permits, you may write to them and inquire about any special etiquette considerations you should know. Telephone inquiries are generally not possible.

Selecting Gift Bearers

Q: How do certain families get chosen to bring up the gifts before Communion during each Mass? It may be silly, but I'm a bit hurt that no one has ever asked our family to participate in this ritual, even though we have attended the same parish regularly for several years. Shouldn't everyone who wishes to do this somehow be included?

A: The specific means for recruiting volunteers to participate in the various aspects of the Mass varies somewhat from parish to parish, often depending upon the size of the parish

and its staff. Sometimes the head usher informally selects someone he knows well at the beginning of Mass, and asks if he or
she will serve as gift bearer for that Mass. Other times, a parish secretary will prepare a list for several months at a time,
assigning volunteers to specific Masses.

At our own parish, a volunteer form is distributed once a
year at all Masses, asking members to designate ways they
would like to become more involved in the worship and ministry of the parish. As a result, the pool of volunteer gift bearers
is so large now that each family only participates about twice
per year. This method involves some paperwork, but is one
way to ensure that all who wish to serve are invited and included.

Call the church office and ask the receptionist or secretary
how the gift-bearer duty is assigned in your parish. Let her
know that you would like to volunteer, and she will certainly
put you in touch with the appropriate person. Contrary to what
you may have thought, this honor is not some kind of "prize"
awarded to the most popular, most attractive, or most devout
members of the parish. All parishes make some attempt to select a variety of willing representatives, but some parishes are
more effective than others at rotating the positions.

Quinceanera Celebration

Q: We received an invitation to a *"quinceanera"* celebration for one of my daughter's friends. It sounds like a big event,
but I really do not understand what it is or how I should respond. The invitation mentions a Mass, although it also seems
to include a dance. Is this a Catholic custom I never encountered before?

A: *Quinceanera* (meaning fifteen years) is a popular tradition among Catholics of Hispanic descent, celebrated when a
daughter reaches fifteen years of age. It's something like a
confirmation and debutante ball rolled into one big (and often
lavish) celebration. Since it is not a custom of the universal

Catholic Church, some American priests try to discourage these festivities. Other priests in areas with large Hispanic populations are more supportive of continuing the tradition.

At the day's Mass, the girl takes part in ceremonies that include leaving her rosary, prayer book, and a bouquet of flowers at Mary's altar. The girl also receives a crown, holy medal, and ring, and renews her baptismal promises. That evening, a dinner, reception, and formal ball usually conclude the celebration.[2]

Appropriate gifts and participation levels vary from community to community and family to family, so it is difficult to offer good guidelines for your situation. Simply contact the girl's family and tell them you're not clear about what the invitation actually entails. Other good local sources of information on this topic may be the parish secretary, your priest, other Hispanic friends, or the manager of a religious-goods store.

Weekend Houseguests

Q: On an upcoming trip, we plan to be weekend houseguests of a devout Protestant family. The last time we visited these friends they included us in their Sunday morning church plans, and gave us no opportunity to seek out a Catholic church. We had no car of our own, and ended up missing Mass and feeling uncomfortable. How can we fulfill our Mass obligation without offending our hosts?

A: Contact your friends and tactfully inquire if Mass attendance is included, or could be included, in your weekend plans. Ideally, you would communicate this request before your arrival to give your hosts time to collect a Mass schedule, and adjust their plans for you accordingly. You could also check the *Official Catholic Directory*,[3] available at many libraries and parish offices, for a listing of Catholic parishes in the area you'll be visiting, or look in the yellow pages under "Churches, Roman Catholic" once you arrive. Let your friends know that you would be happy to attend their church, but would like to attend a Catholic Mass, perhaps on Saturday evening, as well.

You need not apologize for your desire to attend Mass, nor try to explain to them why attending their worship service will not fulfill your Mass obligation. Simply let them know that Mass attendance is an integral part of your life and that you would like to attend Mass with as little inconvenience to them as possible. Hopefully, your friends will respect your request, even if they do not understand it, and help arrange transportation for you.

By the way, when you reciprocate and host these Protestant friends for a weekend at your house, return the consideration by asking them in advance if they wish to attend a local church during their stay.

Undoubtedly, you, as well as I, still have many unanswered questions concerning Catholic etiquette. I trust, however, that the discussion started here will be continued at dinner tables and coffee breaks, and at parishes across the country. God-willing, we may soon begin to see a heightened awareness toward some of these issuess as well as a renewed appreciation for some of the unique aspects of Catholic life.

I hope the information and guidelines I've shared in this book will help you react with added grace and confidence wherever you go. As your religious and social lives intersect, and even collide, may your faith and poise remain unshakable.

Endnotes
1. Mail order sources that offer a selection of distinctly Catholic Christmas cards include: The Thomas More Association, 205 West Monroe St., Chicago, IL 60606; The Printery House, Conception Abbey, Conception, MO 64433; and Abbey Press, St. Meinrad Archabbey, St. Meinrad, IN 47577.
2. Turpin, Joanne, *Catholic Treasures New and Old: Traditions, Customs, and Practices.* St. Anthony Messenger Press, Cincinnati, Ohio: 1994, p. 100.

3. Foy, Felician, O.F.M., and Rose Avato editors, *Our Sunday Visitor's 1996 Catholic Almanac*. Our Sunday Visitor Publishing Division, Huntington, Ind.: 1995, pp. 393-5. A more complete listing appears in *Pilgrims' Guide to America* by J. Anthony Moran. (Our Sunday Visitor Publishing Division: 1992.)

Index

L

M

N

O

Our Sunday Visitor...
Your Source for Discovering the Riches of the Catholic Faith

Our Sunday Visitor has an extensive line of materials for young children, teens, and adults. Our books, Bibles, booklets, CD-ROMs, audios, and videos are available in bookstores worldwide.

To receive a FREE full-line catalog or for more information, call **Our Sunday Visitor** at **1-800-348-2440**. Or write, **Our Sunday Visitor** / 200 Noll Plaza / Huntington, IN 46750.

- -

Please send me: __ A catalog
Please send me materials on:
 __ Apologetics and catechetics __ Reference works
 __ Prayer books __ Heritage and the saints
 __ The family __ The parish

Name_____

Address_____Apt._____

City_____State___Zip_____

Telephone ( )_____

A73BBABP

- -

Please send a friend: __ A catalog
Please send a friend materials on:
 __ Apologetics and catechetics __ Reference works
 __ Prayer books __ Heritage and the saints
 __ The family __ The parish

Name_____

Address_____Apt._____

City_____State___Zip_____

Telephone ( )_____

A73BBABP

- -

Our Sunday Visitor
200 Noll Plaza
Huntington, IN 46750
1-800-348-2440
OSVSALES@AOL.COM

Your Source for Discovering the Riches of the Catholic Faith